D1226736

SCHULER'S

Center Cut Pork Chops with a Dijon Cream Sauce

Schuler's

Fresh Recipes
& Warm Memories

Hans Schuler and Chef Jonathan Schuler

HURON RIVER PRESS

Copyright © 2004 Text and Photography Schuler's Restaurant

All rights reserved. No part of this book may be reproduced in any manner without
the express written consent of the publisher, except in the case of brief excerpts in
critical reviews and articles. All inquiries should be addressed to:

Huron River Press
3622 W. Liberty
Ann Arbor, MI 48103
www.huronriverpress.com

Huron River Press is an imprint of Clock Tower Press, L.L.C.

Design: Savitski Design
Photography: Vaughn Images

Printed and bound in Canada.

10 9 8 7 6 5 4 3 2 1

Library of Congress Cataloging-in-Publication Data

Schuler, Jonathan.
  Schuler's : fresh recipes & warm memories / Jonathan Schuler and Hans Schuler.
    p. cm.
  Includes index.
  ISBN 1-932399-02-X
  1. Cookery, American. 2. Schuler's (Restaurant)—History. I. Schuler, Hans. II. Title.
  TX715.S1455 2004
  641.5973—dc22
                          2003023287

To Jean Schuler *(1913–1973)*

Through the years, many people have played important roles in maintaining and growing our business, and some of those stories are here for you to enjoy. Sometimes, however, the individuals "behind the scenes" play an equally essential role. One such person was my mother, Jean Schuler.

Everyone loved my mother. In many ways, she was the glue that held our family together and the strength behind my father, Win. She gave him the love and support he needed and helped him in every way as he built our family's reputation and expanded the restaurant.

For me, in particular, she was an inspiration—a teacher about life who was my mentor, confidante, and champion all rolled into one. Every son should have such a mother who encourages rather than questions, inspires rather than holds back, loves unconditionally without being overly protective.

Like Will Rogers, she seemed never to meet a person she didn't like. Seven days a week she was there for us with her wit and charm, and we were better for having this thoughtful, giving person among us as a role model. I wouldn't be what I am today, but for her. She'll always be with me, and I'm certain that she would be pleased and proud of how far we've come and of our plans for the future.

— *Hans Schuler*

Jean Schuler used to tell the story about her first Thanksgiving as a member of the Schuler clan. Win and Jean were living in a small house next door to the restaurant, and she had prepared a family feast that included the obligatory turkey. "At 2 p.m., Win came over from the crowded restaurant and took the turkey," said Jean. "A bit later, he sent up a ham as a replacement." The following year, Jean fooled her husband by preparing two turkeys. When, on cue, Win again commandeered the family turkey to meet the needs of the restaurant, Jean brought out the 'bird in reserve,' and the Schuler family had a fine turkey dinner that Thanksgiving, after all!

— *John Collins (Marshall historian)*

Contents

11   All in the Family

13   Marshall: A Hometown

15   A Bit of History

21   Chef's Notes

The Recipes

Stocks, Rubs, and Condiments

24   Chicken Stock

24   Beef Stock

25   Fish Stock

25   Dry Barbecue Rub

26   Creole Seasoning

26   Schuler's BBQ Sauce

27   Basil Pesto

27   Horseradish Cream Sauce

28   Hot Mustard Sauce

29   Herbed Butter

29   Creole Mustard Sauce

30   Garlic and Herb Aioli

30   Spicy Remoulade Sauce

30   Schuler's Seasoning Salt

Salads

32   Brigadoon Salad

32   Curried Chicken Salad with Fresh Fruit and Walnuts

32   Schuler's Salad

34   Duck and Wild Rice Salad

35   Lovers' Salad

35   Michigan Country Apple Salad with Cheddar Cheese and Croutons

37   Grilled Salmon Nicoise

37   Schuler's Famous Cole Slaw

38   Schuler's Garlic House Dressing

38   Maple Syrup Dressing

39   Lemon Herb Vinaigrette

39   Sweet and Sour House Dressing

39   Balsamic Vinaigrette

41   Bitter Green Salad with Sweet Potatoes, Bacon, and Oranges

41   Cantaloupe and Prosciutto with Mixed Greens, Mint, and Mozzarella

42   Seviche and Avocado Salad

Baked Artichoke Hearts with Bread Crumbs and Fresh Herbs

Appetizers and Hors d'Oeuvres

45   Artichoke and Crab Stuffed Mushroom Caps
46   Schuler's Famous Meatballs
47   Schuler's Heritage Cheese Spread
48   Goat Cheese Gratin
48   Prosciutto Cheese Straws
49   Beef Carpaccio and Arugula with
        Lemon Herb Vinaigrette
49   Potted Shrimp
50   Pâté du Maison with a Rhubarb
        Port Wine Reduction
52   House-Made Whole Wheat Crackers
52   Grilled Sourdough Toast Points
52   Garlic Crostini Chips
53   Herbed Focaccia
55   Savory Pesto Cheesecake
56   Baked Artichoke Hearts with Bread Crumbs
        and Fresh Herbs
56   Tapenade Stuffed Cherry Tomatoes
57   Creamy Sautéed Morel Mushrooms
57   Pan-Fried Oysters with Spicy Remoulade Sauce
58   Jalapeño Corn Bread

Sandwiches

61   Roasted Vegetable Panini with Handmade
        Hummus and Feta Cheese
62   Ham and Roast Pork Panini with Pickle and
        Hot Mustard
62   Schuler's Classic Reuben Sandwich
64   Hot Beef Brisket Sandwich with Smoked
        Gouda on Grilled Sourdough
66   Fresh Basil, Tomato, and Camembert on
        Grilled Sourdough
67   Mediterranean-Style Grilled Tuna Steak Hero
68   Chicken and Arugula Sandwich on Focaccia
68   Prime Rib Sandwich with Sweet Onion Relish
        and Maytag Blue Cheese
70   French Dip with Gruyère Cheese

Soups and Stews

73   Schuler's Swiss Onion Soup
73   Midwestern Corn Chowder
74   Schuler's Seafood Chowder
76   Avocado Sweet Potato Vichyssoise
77   Baked Potato Soup
77   Gazpacho
78   Venison Ragout
79   State Fair Lamb Stew
80   Pumpkin Bisque
80   Mushroom Bisque
82   Michigan Bean and Vegetable Soup

Fish and Seafood

84   Blackened Perch with Spicy Remoulade Sauce
84   The Perfect Crab Cake with Creole Mustard Sauce
86   Pan-Fried Tuna Steak with an Asian
        Cucumber Sauce
87   Hazelnut Crusted Walleye
89   Classic Coquille St. Jacques
90   Broiled Whitefish with Herbed Butter
91   Grilled Salmon with Balsamic Vinegar Roasted Beets
92   Halibut en Papillote
93   Lobster Paprikas
94   Lobster and Peas with Saffron Pasta
95   Mussels in a White Wine Broth over Spaghetti
96   Seafood Paella
98   Herb-Stuffed Trout with Horseradish Cream Sauce

Poultry and Meat

100   Center Cut Pork Chops with a Dijon Cream Sauce
101   Marinated Breast of Chicken Dakota
102   Beef Short Ribs Braised in Red Wine
103   Grandma Schuler's Cornish Pasties
104   Cassoulet of Sausages
105   Mediterranean Roast Chicken with
         Pan Braised Potatoes
107   Schuler's Famous Prime Rib
108   Venison Loin with a Cognac Cherry Sauce
109   Filet of Beef with a Cognac Peppercorn Sauce
111   French Bistro Chicken with
         Tarragon Tomato Sauce
112   Oven-Roasted Marinated Leg of Lamb
114   Jonathan's Barbecue Baby Back Ribs
115   New England Pot Roast
115   London Broil
116   Medallions of Veal with Scallions and
         White Wine Sauce
118   Pan Roasted Duck Breast with Winter Vegetables

More...

120   Wild Mushroom Risotto
120   Quiche Lorraine
121   Tortellini a la Crème with Ham and Mushrooms
122   Mushroom Omelet with Herbes de Provence
         and Asiago Cheese
123   Schuler's Signature Lasagna
124   Summertime Vegetable Diablo with
         Angel Hair Pasta
125   Radiator Pasta with Italian Sausage and
         Tomato Basil Cream Sauce
127   Fried Eggplant with Boursin Cheese and
         Sweet Corn Tomato Sauce
128   Pizza Dough
128   Quatro Formaggio Pizza
129   Prosciutto Pizza with Pesto and
         Sun-Dried Tomatoes
129   Smoked Pork Pizza with Barbecue Sauce,
         Cheddar Cheese, and Scallions
130   Rotini Noodles with Shrimp, Red Peppers, and
         Sugar Snap Peas
130   Crustless Spinach and Cheese Pie

Side Dishes

132   Braised Red Cabbage
133   Yorkshire Pudding
133   Yukon Gold Smashed Potatoes with
         Garlic and Chives
135   Roasted Garden Tomatoes
135   Festive Carrot Ring
136   Summer Succotash
136   Cheddar Mashed Potatoes
137   Roasted Asparagus with Pine Nuts
138   Cauliflower with Lemon and Herb Butter
138   Sautéed Summer Squash with Fresh Mint
138   Balsamic Vinegar Roasted Beets with Marjoram
139   Pan Roasted Winter Vegetables
140   Potato Pancakes
140   Spaetzle

Tortellini a la Crème with Ham and Mushrooms

Drinks

143   Jonathan's Soon-To-Be World Famous Margaritas
143   Mojito
143   Simple Syrup
144   Brunchtime Bloody Mary
145   Champagne Cocktail
145   1951 Martini
145   My Favorite Manhattan
148   Party Sangria
151   Brandy Alexander
151   Cosmopolitan
152   Saketini
152   Peach Daiquiri

Desserts

154   Chocolate Bread Pudding with Coffee Liqueur
155   Grandma's Pie Crust
155   Key Lime Pie
157   Coconut Snowball
157   Nighty-Night Cookies
158   Lemon Dream Bars with Raspberry Coulis
160   Coffee Cheesecake
161   Grasshopper Pie
161   Malted Ice Cream
162   Strawberry Rhubarb Pie
163   Peppermint Ribbon Pie
163   Peanut Butter Pie
166   Baked Michigan Apples with
         Homemade Caramel Sauce
167   Michigan Apple Crisp
169   Chocolate Meringue with Fresh Raspberries
         and Whipped Cream
169   Chocolate Silk Pie
170   Strawberry Shortcake with
         Balsamic Vinegar Reduction
171   South Haven Blueberry Cobbler

173   Back to the Future

175   Acknowledgments

177   Index

Grasshopper Pie

Centennial Room fireplace

All in the Family

by Keith Kehlbeck

No matter what the business, 95 years is a long time. When Albert Schuler Sr. opened a restaurant on Main Street of Marshall, Michigan in 1909, Ty Cobb and Honus Wagner were stars in the National Pastime. William Howard Taft was President. The term "World War" had not yet been coined (let alone twice). And not only was the information superhighway nonexistent, the interstate *highway* system was five decades from fruition.

For 95 years, Schuler's Restaurant & Pub has kept it in the family— and beaten the odds. How rare is this achievement? According to the Family Firm Institute (FFI), nearly 70 percent of all family owned businesses fail before reaching the second generation, and 88 percent fail before the third generation. Only about 3 percent survive to the fourth generation and beyond.

The Royal Hotel and Restaurant, purchased by Albert Schuler in 1924 and re-named "Schuler's."

Each of the four generations of Schuler's—while presenting strikingly different styles—has helped to build a family reputation and traditions that involve good, honest work and a love of food, people, and the community. Along the way, each, in their own way, has shown a flair for imagination and innovation in the hospitality and food industry.

An orphaned cigar-maker who became a restaurant owner, hotelier and peace officer, Albert Schuler loved to cook. He passed along that passion to his sons, along with the building blocks for a hospitality dynasty.

Winston Schuler, an exceptional collegiate athlete, had wanted to teach and possibly coach sports. After a stint in the Navy during World War II, he returned to the family business in Marshall. Over nearly 50 years, he would turn the family name into a household word in the Midwest and become a popular icon.

Groomed for the business and determined to modernize and improve while staying true to the family philosophy, Hans Schuler learned many different aspects of the job as a young man. His vision for the future has helped to perpetuate the restaurant's success.

Larry Schuler has continued in the family business as owner of Schu's Restaurant in St. Joseph, Michigan, and, like his grandfather, has served as President of the Michigan Restaurant Association. Hans's other son, Jonathan, like his great-grandfather, loves to work in the kitchen. With refreshing new culinary approaches, he continues the traditions of excellence for which the Schuler name is known.

These men are very different, yet each has had a role to play in the family's traditions. "Grandfather started it all, Dad built and

Schuler's first outdoor advertising. Albert Schuler successfully ran for county sheriff in 1939.

enhanced the image. My sons have embraced fine food and hospitality in their careers. We're happy to be carrying on the tradition while working to meet the needs and desires of America's dining public," says Hans Schuler.

Some of the recipes contained in this book are new; others are old favorites. In many ways, they reflect the diversity and creativity that have been a part of the Schuler family experience for 95 years. This is the story of a restaurant that has continued to evolve as it approaches a century of service to its guests. And, it's the story of a family, whose love for fine food and drink has made that evolution possible.

Marshall: A Home Town

In his book, *A History of Marshall,* Richard Carver describes how a small settlement along old Indian, fur trader, and stagecoach routes grew from a log house with a few intrepid pioneers in 1831 to a bustling community of businesses and historic houses that today sits along the interstate roughly equidistant between Chicago and Detroit.

Today, Marshall—named after the Supreme Court justice who pioneered American jurisprudence—is a quintessential American small town of approximately 7,000 souls. It is known for several things. Locals will tell you that the town missed becoming the capital of the state of Michigan by a single vote in the state legislature. And every fall, thousands of visitors from throughout the region come to the city's Historic Home Tour, which features an extraordinary selection of restored homes, many within its National Historic Landmark District boundaries.

At the turn of the last century, while known as a transportation hub and manufacturing center, Marshall also had more than its share of establishments dedicated to gustatory pleasures and the needs of travelers. Carver reports that, in 1894, Marshall boasted 19 saloons, clubs, and lodges, and an even greater number of hotels and boarding-houses.

For many Midwesterners, however, Marshall has become synonymous with Schuler's Restaurant, the flagship establishment that has been credited with making Marshall a nationally known destination for dining and tourism. Perhaps it is no coincidence that Marshall's nickname is "The City of Hospitality." An article in the 1960s reported that, "In a town of 6,000, Schuler's feeds 400,000 people a year, serves 5,500 pounds of beef and 1,500 pounds of seafood each week." Today, the restaurant is doing better than ever, although dining patterns and lifestyles have changed.

As an employer, civic participant, and drawing card for tourists, Schuler's has a vested interest in this small Midwestern community.

Photographs of "Historic Marshall" adorn the walls of Schuler's Centennial Room, and, as a local employer, corporate citizen, and destination point for visitors throughout the region, the restaurant continues to be an important part of the vibrant downtown of this Midwestern community.

Albert W. Schuler Sr. started the family business in 1909.

A Bit of History

It all started with a lunch counter.

America, at the turn of the twentieth century, was a cauldron of entrepreneurship. Immigration and the Industrial Revolution had changed communities throughout the country—nowhere more so than in the Midwest. In cities and towns like Marshall, Michigan, businesses and commerce began to cater to a diverse population that increasingly liked to travel and to be entertained.

As a youth, Albert Schuler worked as a delivery boy in the local grocery store. Lacking a trade, he became a cigar-maker—ironically, the line of work his biological father was reported to have pursued. Cigar-making appears to have been a popular vocation in this small Michigan community. An early Marshall business gazetteer lists over 50 types of cigars that were produced locally.

In 1909 Albert started a cigar store, and soon added billiard tables, a bakery, and a lunch counter. As an additional venture he purchased the Garrick Café in 1917, which he operated with a partner. The specialty of Albert's 30-seat eatery was a 25-cent blue plate dinner.

In 1920 he purchased a hotel with a small dining room on Main Street, and named it The Albert. By 1924, with $5,000 in savings as a down payment, Albert was ready to expand his business because "you can't raise four kids on the salary of a deputy sheriff"— an office to which he had been appointed while operating the Garrick Café. He sold the hotel on Main Street, purchased the larger Royal Hotel and Restaurant, and immediately changed the name to Schuler's.

Where it all began—Albert Schuler's original dining room on Main Street, Marshall, circa 1909.

In his capacity as deputy sheriff it wasn't unusual for Albert to be summoned to attend to matters of the law. In such cases the restauranteur/hotelier-turned-peace officer would take off his apron and was out the door. Minutes (or hours) later, his apron was back on and it was business as usual.

Perhaps more than anything, Albert loved to cook. He noted later that he "always set a good table" for his family. That love of cooking carried over to the restaurant—and in many ways was passed along to his sons.

Albert's son, Winston (or "Win") got an early introduction to the rigors of the hospitality industry and developed a healthy work ethic that would last his entire life. At age 14, he rose at 5:30 A.M. to cook before heading to school. He was his father's hotel night clerk, but was always paid for his work, which allowed him to save some extra money. As a result, the enterprising young man had $1,000 in his pocket when he set off for college. While attending nearby Albion College, Win worked as a waiter in the fraternity house. After a stellar athletic career at Albion, he graduated in 1930 and took a teaching and coaching job in Wakefield, a small community in Michigan's Upper Peninsula.

In 1934 Albert Schuler let his son know that he was ready to turn over the management of the hotel to someone else. "I'm tired," he told Winston. "You're either going to take this over or I'm going to find some other young fellow." The lure of the family business proved to be enough for Win to come home to Marshall. Win gave up teaching to concentrate on the business full time, and with his brother, Albert Jr., was given the task of

Schuler's Bowling Alley in 1937; now Winston's Pub and the Centennial Room

running the hotel's restaurant. A seven-lane bowling alley was added, and Schuler's became a popular gathering spot for locals and visitors.

After serving as an officer in the Navy during World War II, Win returned to Marshall for good.

In 1954 he bought out his brother's share of the restaurant, and began to popularize his brand of hospitality. A man with a natural flair for showmanship—who became known as "the consummate host"—Win left an indelible mark on the hospitality industry over the next four decades.

Meanwhile, Schuler's reputation grew. In 1952 the restaurant won the first of 37 consecutive Travel Holiday Fine Dining Awards. Over the years other recognition followed. In 1971 Win was awarded the prestigious Gold Plate Award as the National Food Service Operator of the Year, and that same year, Schuler's was selected as one of 10 "restaurateurs of distinction" for the first annual Ivy Award, an honor conveyed by colleagues and competitors in the food service industry. *Cooking for Profit* and *Restaurant Business* included Schuler's among their "Top 100" American restaurants. Most importantly, as one newspaper noted, "word-of-mouth spread the Schuler name," and guests flocked to the restaurant, spurred on by recommendations from family members and acquaintances who loved the food, ambience, and service for which Schuler's had become famous.

In 1959 Win's son, Hans, had become the third generation to join the family business, and he was running the company by the 1970s. In 1982 Win retired as Chairman of the Board, and Hans took the reins of a regional and national destination. Building on that legacy was a challenge he relished.

Schuler's celebrates its 75th anniversary in 1984. Hans, Larry, and Win examine a new promotional piece.

Hans Schuler had grown up in the business. Like his father, he worked in the restaurant at an early age. Family lore has it that when Hans was three years old he was asked to carry the restaurant's money sack, but dropped it on the way to the bank. (Someone found it and came running into the bank with it.) That early miscue notwithstanding, Hans was born to be an entrepreneur. As a young man he was assigned responsibilities that would provide an in-depth understanding of what it means to run a successful restaurant. Like all Schuler family members, he started on the dish machine affectionately christened "the China Clipper." When he was 12 years old, he was shucking shrimp. At 15 he was working in the restaurant's butcher shop, and often ran the broiler and cooked. Later he managed the restaurant commissary and plant operation. "Essentially, I worked every job in the place," says Hans. "I doubled as a host when needed."

Hans originally attended Cornell University but transferred to Michigan State University, where he received his degree in hotel, restaurant, and institutional management. Upon his graduation he was ready to assume a more active role in the family business and to assist in running the Marshall operations. Named president of the company in 1970, he was increasingly responsible for major expansions, ongoing renovations, and supervising the business decisions that would take Schuler's into the twenty-first century. Chief among these were the sale of the Bar-Scheeze food division to Campbell's Soup in 1982 and the decision to concentrate the corporation's efforts in the flagship restaurant—where it all started.

| A Schuler Timeline | 1909 Albert Schuler Sr. opens a combination cigar store and restaurant in Marshall, Michigan. | 1924 Albert purchases the Royal Hotel and Restaurant and renames it Schuler's. | 1936 Albert hands over the restaurant to his sons Albert Jr. and Winston. | 1952 Win Schuler's Bar-Scheeze is introduced in the restaurant and the bar. | 1959 Hans Schuler, Win's son, graduates from Michigan State University and joins the family business. |

Along the way, he found time to be a quiet contributor to the local and regional community where he lives and works. Starting locally by serving on the Chamber Board (and being recognized as Marshall Young Man of the Year), he eventually expanded his focus to the state, where he served as Chairman of Michigan Week for the Greater Michigan Foundation and chaired the Governor's Annual Conference on Tourism. He has been a member of the AAA Michigan Board of Directors since 1978, and was the group's chairman in 1989 and 1990. Service on many civic community boards demonstrates his interest in "giving back" to the state and region that have supported the restaurant through the years.

Hans' oldest son, Larry, followed in the family business by managing and then owning Schuler's operations outside of Marshall, including the more informal Schu's in St. Joseph.

The youngest Schuler son, Jonathan, also developed a love for cooking. "In cooking, I do what I'm excited about," says Jonathan. "I don't cater to a specific market or trend. What's important to me is that I *do something special* when I'm creating a new dish." Great-grandfather Albert couldn't have said it any better. Largely self-taught—with a brief stint in a culinary school—Jonathan has developed his own style and skills in the marketplace. Taking a job as an Executive Chef with Creative Dining Service, he has continued to hone his skills and, with his older brother and father, brings the family full circle to what began nearly a century ago at a lunch counter in Marshall. ◆

1968 Hans refines the secret Bar-Scheeze formula, registers its trademark, and introduces the popular product in supermarkets for the first time.

1971 In the first year that the awards are given by the restaurant industry, Schuler's receives the national Ivy Award for Excellence.

1973 Albert Schuler passes away.

1977 Win Schuler's of Marshall is proclaimed a Michigan Historic Site.

1987 Restaurant receives Restaurant Business' "Top 100 Award," and is Three-Diamond rated by AAA.

1993 Win Schuler passes away.

1997 Schuler's recognized as a Michigan Centennial Business.

Chef's Note

When I think about the inevitability of my career as a chef, I laugh at how defiantly I resisted it. I went to college intent on being an attorney, and I might have been a success if it hadn't been for all the schoolwork. I tried investment advising, steel sales, painting houses, and even worked in a hotel, all under the pretense of choosing my own fate rather than simply following in my family's footsteps. I bombed at everything.

After several years, I found myself in the kitchen, but only as a side trip. I enrolled in culinary school as a way to pass the time while I decided what I wanted to be when I grew up…and loved it! Still, I pretended to ignore the warning signs that I would soon be trading in my dress shirts for chef whites. It seems it was obvious to everyone but me that cooking was the only thing I'd ever be good at.

Once I realized that the world would not spin off its axis if I returned to the family career, I gave in, reluctantly at first, but finally with the zeal of the born-again. I finally understood what a fortunate childhood I had, and how much Schuler's restaurant meant to me growing up. I gained a new respect for the memories of my youth: working in the restaurant for my father, cooking with my mother,

and listening to my grandfather, Win, share his pearls of wisdom about exceeding customers' expectations. I remembered events with a clarity I wouldn't have valued or appreciated had I not struck out on my own.

So I've come full circle, returning to my culinary roots and working with my father. This book, which is a result of my father's dedication to the family business, reflects the melding of his legacy and my cooking style: a solid foundation with an eye for experimentation. I like to compare our efforts to working on a grand historic home. The foundation may be solid, the façade still beautiful, but in need of subtle changes. Rather than razing the house, you're better off renovating, updating, improving. That's why I agreed to work on this cookbook with my dad. It was time to celebrate our family recipes, while updating them for today's palate. I hope you'll enjoy them and experiment so they become your own.

From our family to yours,

— *Jonathan Schuler*

Besides barbecue meatballs—a longtime Schuler's favorite—appetizers over the years have included such things as marinated herring, green peas and peanuts with mayonnaise, sauerkraut with caraway, crisp raw vegetables and a lazy-Susan relish tray. Probably the most well-known "nibble stuff," however, was Schuler's "Bar-Scheeze," a concoction of cheese and beer that Win Schuler developed in 1952 to provide something for the

SCHMEER ON SOME SCHEEZE

guests to immediately have at their table when they arrived. "Dad originally called it Beer Cheese,'" says Hans Schuler, "but we decided on the more trademarkable 'Bar-Scheeze,' which also is a play on the Schuler name." ◆ "Bar-Scheeze"—a name that was popularized at the restaurant and that Hans Schuler promoted nationally—went through several changes as a product. In the early days, the mixing of the ingredients was done in a washing machine, using the agitator to fold the cheese to spreadable consistency. The product included fresh horseradish and Worcestershire sauce in addition to the primary ingredients of beer and cheese. "Duffy" Daugherty, Michigan State football coach, friend of Win Schuler's and the unofficial early "taster" for the cheese and beer mixture, recommended that Win buy some stoneware crocks for the spread. Coach Daugherty also

had a keen appreciation for the complexities of quality control. "When you're eating cheese and drinking beer, you'd better come out even," said Duffy. ◆ Soon Bar-Scheeze was being produced in a small "plant" by six people who "more or less" followed Win's recipe, combining beer and cheese in equal portions to provide a spreading consistency for the cheese. "More of the beer ended up in the employees than in the cheese," observed Hans Schuler, who set out to standardize and enlarge production of the cheese. ◆ The popular spread soon became the first thing people talked about when they discussed Schuler's. A *Wall Street Journal* ad led to mail orders, and Win Schuler's "Bar-Scheeze" eventually came to be served on United Airlines flights. In 1982 the name and product were sold to Campbell Soup Company, and consumers continue to find the product in grocery stores throughout the Midwest. Today, a slightly different but no less tasty cheese spread still appears on the tables at Schuler's—Heritage Cheese Spread. ◆ "People come to a restaurant because they're hungry, so get some food out," Albert had advised his son years before. Today's Heritage Cheese spread, crackers, and fresh-baked bread—like "Bar-Scheeze" in the past—fit the bill and continue to provide a little something extra for guests when they sit down at the table.

Stocks, Rubs, and Condiments

Chicken Stock

3   tablespoons unsalted butter
I   tablespoon virgin olive oil
2   large carrots, peeled and roughly chopped
I   large onion, roughly chopped
2   stalks celery, roughly chopped
5   whole garlic cloves
I   cup dry white wine
6   sprigs thyme
6   sprigs parsley
6   basil leaves
2   bay leaves
I   tablespoon black peppercorns, toasted
3-4 pounds chicken bones, wings, backs, and/or necks
I   gallon cold water
Makes 2 quarts

I Heat the butter and olive oil in a large stockpot over medium heat. When the butter begins to foam, add the carrots, onion, celery, and garlic. Sauté the vegetables, stirring occasionally, until golden brown, about 10 minutes. Add the white wine and stir, then add the herbs, peppercorns, chicken bones, and water and bring just to a simmer. Turn the heat to low and skim off any impurities that have risen to the surface. Simmer for 2 and ½ hours. Strain through a colander lined with cheesecloth and refrigerate or freeze until ready to use. This stock will only last 2–3 days in the refrigerator.

Beef Stock

3   pounds veal or beef bones, sawed into 2-inch pieces
2   pounds stew beef, cut into 1½-inch cubes
¼   cup tomato paste
I   large onion, quartered
2   carrots, quartered
2   ribs of celery, quartered
5   peeled whole garlic cloves
4   sprigs parsley
2   sprigs thyme
2   sprigs basil
I   bay leaf
I   gallon plus I cup of cold water
Makes 2 quarts

I Preheat oven to 450°.

2 Spread the bones and beef in a roasting pan and roast them for 30 minutes, or until the bones are brown. Using tongs, transfer the bones and meat to a large stockpot. Pour off the excess fat from the pan and add 1 cup of water in order to scrape the brown bits from the bottom; add to the stockpot.

3 Add the tomato paste, onion, carrots, celery, herbs, and water and bring to a low boil. Turn the heat to low and skim off any impurities that have risen to the surface. Simmer for 4–6 hours. Strain through a colander lined with cheesecloth and refrigerate or freeze until ready to use.

Fish Stock

1	tablespoon unsalted butter
1	medium onion, chopped
1	carrot, chopped
1	celery, chopped
3	pounds fish bones and heads, rinsed well
1	bay leaf
1	bunch parsley stems
2	sprigs fresh thyme
4	cups cold water
1	cup dry white wine

Makes 1 quart

1 Melt the butter in the bottom of a stockpot. Add the onion, carrot, and celery and sauté until soft. Add the fish bones, herbs, water, and wine and bring to a low boil. Turn down the heat and simmer for 20 minutes.

2 Strain through a colander lined with cheesecloth and refrigerate until ready to use.

This rub can be used on pork ribs, chops, or beef brisket. The sweet taste combined with the hickory and apple wood smoke from the smoker provides a taste you will not soon forget.

Dry Barbecue Rub

¼	cup brown sugar
4	teaspoons onion powder
1	teaspoon ground cinnamon
1	teaspoon dry mustard
1	teaspoon kosher salt
½	teaspoon dry thyme
1	teaspoon celery salt
1	teaspoon chili powder

1 Combine all the ingredients in a bowl. Rub liberally into pork ribs. Let the ribs stand in the rub for at least two hours before smoking. The ingredients can be stored in an airtight container for a week or two. This recipe is about enough for two full racks of ribs.

WHAT'S IN A NAME? In German, the name Schuler means "scholar" or "student." It's a common name, and, ironically, one that the first generation of Marshall Schulers chose, rather than inherited. Albert Schuler Sr. or "Bert" was seven years old when his mother died and his father left him with neighbors and moved on. An itinerant butcher named Schuler took in the boy, and, while not formally adopted, Albert later took the name as his own. Today, "Schuler's of Marshall" has come to represent the finest traditions of dining and hospitality, and the name is recognized far and wide. ◆ Years later, Albert's son Winston (right) would welcome guests named Schuler, who oftentimes would ask, "Are we related?" "If you embrace me, I'll embrace you," Win would say.

This seasoning mix is used in the Crab Cake recipe and the Blackened Perch recipe.
Feel free to experiment with it in other dishes and sauces that need some extra oomph!
The cayenne pepper provides the heat here, so vary that ingredient to your preference.

Creole Seasoning

⅓   cup table salt
¼   cup granulated or powdered garlic
¼   cup freshly ground black pepper
2   tablespoons cayenne pepper, or to taste
2   tablespoons dried thyme
2   tablespoons dried basil
2   tablespoons dried oregano
2   tablespoons dried tarragon
⅓   cup paprika
3   tablespoons granulated or powdered onion
Makes about 2 cups

I   Combine all the ingredients in a medium-sized bowl. Ingredients can be stored in an airtight container for several weeks.

This is the sweet and smoky sauce for which Schuler's is known. Traditionally, it's served
with our famous meatballs, but it makes a terrific sauce for baby back pork ribs as well.

Schuler's BBQ Sauce

I   teaspoon salt
½   cup granulated sugar
¼   cup brown sugar
3   cups Beef Stock (pg 24)
½   cup prepared mustard
¼   cup white vinegar
⅛   cup liquid smoke
½   cup Worcestershire sauce
I   cup ketchup
Makes I quart

I   Combine all the ingredients and simmer in heavy kettle for two hours, uncovered. Stir often so it does not burn.

This is the classic sauce that is tossed with fresh pasta to make a quick and delicious meal. I love to use it as a pizza sauce. See, for example, the Prosciutto Pizza with Pesto and Sun-Dried Tomatoes. This sauce is also a key ingredient in the Savory Pesto Cheesecake.

Basil Pesto

4	cups packed fresh basil leaves, washed well
½	cup pine nuts, toasted until golden, cooled and chopped fine
½	cup freshly grated Parmesan (about 1½ ounces)
2	large garlic cloves, minced
¼	cup extra-virgin olive oil

Makes 1¼ cup

I In a food processor, puree the basil with the remaining ingredients until smooth and season with salt and pepper. Pesto can be made 2 days ahead and chilled (cover with plastic wrap).

This sauce is a great accompaniment to prime rib. It is even better when making one of those day-after prime rib sandwiches.

Horseradish Cream Sauce

¾	cup heavy whipping cream
½	cup mayonnaise
½	cup prepared horseradish
2	tablespoons Dijon mustard
	Pinch sugar
	Salt and freshly ground pepper to taste

Makes 3 cups

I Whip the cream separately and fold into the other ingredients already combined. Salt and pepper to taste.

sense is not so common.

— Voltaire

One teaspoon of my mom's Hot Mustard Sauce on the Ham and Roast Pork Panini
will clear out your sinuses. But don't be intimidated…the flavor is out of this world!

Hot Mustard Sauce

1	cup malt vinegar
1	cup dry mustard
3	egg yolks
1	cup sugar

Makes 2½ cups

1 Soak the vinegar and dry mustard together in a glass or stainless steel bowl overnight. Whisk the egg yolks and sugar and heat over double boiler, whisking constantly, until thick, about 10 minutes. Store in the refrigerator or freezer.

WHERE EVERYBODY KNOWS YOUR NAME… Long before television's Cheers bar was the place where "everybody knows your name, and everyone's glad you came," Schuler's epitomized the type of place where preferential treatment was the norm, and guests were personally acknowledged by the owner. ◆ One of the most important aspects of being a consummate host was remembering people's names. Win's memory for recalling names and faces of customers was legendary. After years of habit, he became adept at recalling some association with a person that released the customer's name from his memory bank. He also used different methods to imprint customers in his memory, including a crib sheet with a layout of the dining room, notes on what guests liked to drink, and even "eavesdropping." ◆ It became a sort of game for Win (at left, standing). "I'd keep a pad in my pocket and write everything down…who people were and what they did. Then I'd review the whole thing every night." ◆ Demonstrating that personal hospitality is still the norm, Hans Schuler remains very active in the restaurant. He and his managers readily "make the rounds" to greet customers, new and old. More than anything else, those personal greetings make the Schuler's experience memorable.

Herbed Butter

2   sticks butter, softened
     Dash Worcestershire sauce
     Dash brandy
½   teaspoon Dijon mustard
1   green onion, finely diced
1   tablespoon basil, finely chopped
2   cloves garlic, crushed
1   teaspoon capers, finely chopped
1   tablespoon red onion, finely chopped
½   teaspoon dried thyme
     Salt and white pepper to taste
     Makes 8 servings

1 Using the paddle attachment on your mixer, beat the butter until it becomes pale. Add the remainder of the ingredients and beat until well mixed.

2 With a spatula, transfer all of the contents of the bowl to a sheet of parchment paper. Roll up the parchment and twist off the ends to form the butter into the shape of a log. Place the log in freezer bag and store in the freezer. Cut off round disks of butter as you need them. The butter will keep for a couple of months, at least.

Creole Mustard Sauce

½   cup heavy cream
½   cup dairy sour cream
6   tablespoons Creole mustard or Colman's brown mustard
⅛   teaspoon Creole Seasoning (pg 26)
2   teaspoons Worcestershire sauce
1   teaspoon prepared mustard
     Makes about 1½ cups

1 Whisk all the ingredients together over medium-low heat in a sturdy saucepan. Stir regularly for 20 minutes or until the sauce thickens. Serve hot or at room temperature.

Garlic and Herb Aioli

½ cup mayonnaise
¼ cup sour cream
1 tablespoon minced fresh parsley
1 teaspoon minced fresh rosemary
3 cloves minced garlic
2 tablespoons fresh lemon juice
Makes about 1 cup

I Mix all ingredients thoroughly.
Put this spread on almost any kind
of sandwich or serve it as a sauce
with chicken, fish, or poached eggs.

Spicy Remoulade Sauce

2 cups mayonnaise
2 tablespoons fresh squeezed lemon juice
1 teaspoon capers
1 teaspoon anchovies
1 teaspoon gherkins
1 teaspoon fresh parsley
1 teaspoon fresh tarragon
1 teaspoon Dijon mustard
Makes about 2¼ cups

I Finely dice the capers, anchovies,
gherkins, parsley, and tarragon.
Mix all ingredients well.

Schuler's Seasoning Salt

1 cup kosher salt
1 tablespoon black pepper
1 tablespoon ground rosemary
1 teaspoon garlic powder
1 teaspoon celery seed
1 teaspoon dried thyme leaves
Makes 1¼ cup

I Mix all ingredients together with a
wire whisk and store in an airtight
jar. Keep the salt handy by the stove
to season steaks, chops, or roasts.

Salads

Brigadoon Salad

1	cup iceberg lettuce
½	cup fresh spinach
½	cup romaine lettuce
½	cup diced fresh pineapple
½	cup fresh sliced strawberries
3	raw button mushrooms, sliced
4	ounces chilled salad shrimp
2	ounces toasted almonds
3	ounces Sweet and Sour House Dressing (pg 39)

Serves 2

1 Mound the iceberg, spinach and romaine onto each of two salad plates. Arrange the pineapples, strawberries, mushrooms, and shrimp attractively over each mound.

2 Sprinkle with the toasted almonds and drizzle with dressing. Serve immediately.

Curried Chicken Salad with Fresh Fruit and Walnuts

1	pound grilled chicken breast meat, diced
1	Granny Smith apple, cored but unpeeled, cut into ¼ inch cubes
1	cup red grapes, halved
1	cup celery, finely chopped
½	cup chopped walnuts, toasted
½	cup mayonnaise
1½	teaspoon Horseradish Cream Sauce (pg 27)
1	teaspoon Madras curry powder
½	teaspoon celery seed
	Kosher salt and fresh ground pepper to taste

Serves 6

1 Chill the chicken and mayonnaise before mixing. Whisk the mayonnaise, horseradish cream, curry powder, celery seed, and salt and pepper together separately.

2 Combine with the chicken, apples, grapes, walnuts, and celery in a large bowl. To enhance the flavor, keep the salad covered in the refrigerator for at least 2 hours before serving.

3 Serve on a buttery croissant with a tender leaf of Bibb lettuce.

Schuler's Salad

1	cup chopped iceberg lettuce
½	cup chopped spinach leaves
½	cup chopped romaine leaves
1	ounce crumbled bacon bits
1	ounce bleu cheese crumbles
4	ounces shredded Swiss cheese
6	grape tomatoes
8	whole black olives
4	cucumber slices
2	ounces Schuler's Garlic House Dressing (pg 38)

Serves 2

1 Mound the salad greens in the center of two ice-cold plates. Sprinkle each serving with shredded Swiss cheese and top with bacon bits and bleu cheese crumbles.

2 Garnish with tomatoes, black olives, and cucumbers. Drizzle with the dressing and serve.

Brigadoon Salad

The meaty flavor of the duck combined with the sweetness of the maple syrup dressing
will appeal to almost any palate. This dish serves four if the duck breasts are large
(10–12 ounces). If the breasts are smaller, use four duck breasts and serve one per person.

Duck and Wild Rice Salad

2   duck breast halves with skin
2   cups wild rice
3   tablespoons unsalted butter
1   medium onion, finely chopped
6   cups Chicken Stock (pg 24)
4   oz Maple Syrup Dressing (pg 38)
6   scallions
1   large Granny Smith apple, unpeeled and diced
1   cup moist dried apricots, diced
1½ cups toasted pecans
1   teaspoon kosher salt
1   head Bibb lettuce and 2 cups frisee lettuce for garnish
    Makes 4 dinner salads

1 Preheat oven to 375°.

2 Start with the rice, because it will take the longest. Rinse wild rice in a sieve under cold water and drain. Heat butter in a large heavy pot over medium heat, add the onions, and cook until golden brown, about 5 minutes.

3 Add the rice and cook, stirring, until fragrant, about 3 minutes. Add the chicken stock and simmer, covered, until the rice has split open and most of the liquid has been absorbed, about 1 hour to 1 hour 15 minutes. (If you need to make the dressing, this would be the time to whisk the ingredients together, while the rice is cooking.) Drain the rice when done.

4 Season the duck breast halves with salt and pepper. Score the duck in a crosshatch pattern, being careful not to cut into the skin. Place the duck skin-side up in an oiled roasting pan and put into the oven for about 20 minutes, or until medium rare (about 125° on a meat thermometer).

5 Take the breasts from the oven and remove the skins. Let the meat rest while you thinly slice the skins and return them to the oven. Cook the skins until they are crisp.

6 Next, chop the scallions, apples, and apricots and add them to the dressing with the drained rice and the toasted pecans. Toss everything gently together and salt and pepper to taste.

7 Slice the duck breasts thinly across the grain on a cutting board in preparation for service. To serve, line a dinner plate with the Bibb and frisée lettuce, mound the rice mixture in the middle and place the duck breasts and the crispy skin on the top.

8 Serve with a nice pinot noir or a peppery zinfandel.

You may delay, but time will

— Ben Franklin

My grandpa Win would often duck back into the kitchen to create this first course himself
for a couple enjoying a romantic evening together. I can just see him now delivering his
handiwork with a wink, pointing out that the salad was only good for a few hours!

Lovers' Salad

1   cup chopped iceberg lettuce
½   cup chopped fresh spinach
½   cup chopped romaine lettuce
1   large hard-boiled egg, chopped
1   ounce crumbled bacon
4   mushroom caps, sliced
2   tablespoons toasted almonds
4   fresh strawberries, sliced
2   ounces Sweet and Sour
    House Dressing (pg 39)
Serves 2

1   Don't get too fixated on the exact
quantities for the ingredients in this
recipe. Part of the fun is to add extra
bacon or strawberries into the recipe
if that's what you like.

2   Start with a mound of lettuce in the
middle of two plates (this is a lovers'
salad, after all!) and arrange the other
ingredients over the top however you
like. Drizzle with the dressing and serve!

This is a fresh and simple way to enjoy the fall apple harvest in your home area.
I've found this salad to make a great lunch or a terrific first course for a sit-down dinner.

Michigan Country Apple Salad with Cheddar Cheese and Croutons

1   cup croutons
4   ounces Maple Syrup Dressing (pg 38)
2   cups Michigan apples (Try your favorite.
    Mine are Jonathans—of course!)
½   pound mixed baby greens
1   cup shredded sharp cheddar cheese
Serves 4

1   If you want to prepare your own
croutons, simply cut up some stale
bread, toss with a small amount of
salad oil, dried thyme, and salt and
pepper, and bake at 350° until
golden brown.

2   Prepare the Maple Syrup Dressing.
Core and slice your apples, leaving
the peels on, and toss with the dressing to keep them from browning.
In a large mixing bowl combine the
greens, shredded cheddar cheese,
and croutons.

3   Pour the apples and the dressing
over the top and toss to combine.
Place a mound on each plate and
serve immediately.

not.

Grilled Salmon Nicoise

This has been a popular salad on the menu at Schuler's. Have some friends over for lunch at your house and try serving this dish family style on a beautiful serving platter for a dramatic visual presentation. Consider doing as the French do by serving it with a glass of nouveau Beaujolais and a crusty baguette.

Grilled Salmon Nicoise

¾   pound green beans, trimmed

1½   pound Yukon Gold or redskin potatoes, halved

4   six-ounce salmon fillets

1   teaspoon kosher salt

Freshly ground black pepper

Vegetable oil for brushing

¼   cup drained bottled capers

¾   pound Bibb lettuce (2 heads), leaves separated and large ones torn into pieces

1   pint grape tomatoes

4   oz Lemon Herb Vinaigrette Dressing (pg 39)

⅔   cup Nicoise or other small brine-cured black olives

4   hard-boiled large eggs, quartered

3   tablespoons finely chopped fresh parsley and/or basil

Serves 4

1 Cook the beans and potatoes in separate 4- to 6-quart pots of boiling salted water, uncovered, until crisp-tender. The potatoes will take at least 5 minutes longer than the beans.

2 When the beans are done, remove them with tongs and shock them in a bowl of ice water to stop them from cooking. When the potatoes are done, simply drain them and let them cool.

3 Brush the salmon with oil and sprinkle the fillets with kosher salt and ground black pepper. Grill over a medium hot flame on your grill or under a broiler until they are browned on the outside but still pink in the center.

4 Toss the beans, potatoes, lettuce leaves, and tomatoes separately with a splash of the dressing. Mound the lettuce in the center of a serving platter.

5 Arrange the beans, potatoes, hard-boiled eggs, tomatoes, olives, and capers around the edge, in sundial fashion. Place the grilled salmon fillets over the top, sprinkle with fresh parsley, and drizzle with the remaining dressing.

Schuler's Famous Cole Slaw

One large head cabbage

One peeled and grated carrot

3   cups whipping cream

⅓   cup sugar

⅓   cup cider vinegar

1   teaspoon caraway seeds

1   teaspoon celery seeds

Kosher salt and fresh ground pepper to taste

Serves 8

1 Peel and clean the head of cabbage, making sure to remove all of the tough outer leaves. Slice the cabbage into as-thin-as-possible julienne strips. I use a knife, but a mandolin is ideal for this as well. Combine with grated carrot in a large bowl.

2 Separately, mix the vinegar, sugar, caraway, and celery seeds together in a small bowl. Whip the cream until stiff in a medium size bowl. Add the vinegar mixture to the cream and fold together with a spatula.

3 Add this mixture to a large bowl with the cabbage and toss together. Salt and pepper to taste. Store in the refrigerator until ready to serve.

Schuler's Garlic House Dressing

½ cup mayonnaise
½ cup vegetable oil
½ cup apple cider vinegar
2 tablespoons sugar
3-4 cloves garlic, crushed
    Salt and pepper to taste
    Makes 1½ cups

1 Whisk all the ingredients together and store covered in refrigerator until ready to use.

Maple Syrup Dressing

3 tablespoons maple syrup
¼ cup apple cider vinegar
3 tablespoons fresh orange juice
1 teaspoon Dijon mustard
1 teaspoon mild honey
½ cup vegetable oil
½ teaspoon kosher salt
½ teaspoon freshly ground black pepper
    Enough for 4 dinner salads

1 Combine the maple syrup, vinegar, orange juice, mustard, and honey in a small bowl. Add the oil in a steady stream, whisking constantly. Season with salt and pepper.

SOMETHING SPECIAL FOR YOU... Whether it was a unique appetizer, a special sauce or salad dressing, or simply a "not on the menu" item prepared for a guest, Schuler's became known for pleasing its customers with that "extra" something that made the meal memorable. ◆ Win Schuler often prepared dishes that didn't appear on the menu, but were his personal favorites. A food critic at the time noted that Win and his managers "each tries to create a special dish, so that if he knows a guest has come some distance to eat, he can say, 'please give me the privilege of arranging a little different first course for you, and perhaps a different salad, with my compliments'." ◆ Over the years, certain "special" items became staples of the restaurant. The "Lovers' Salad," for example, received particular attention from customers and the staff alike. "Never served to unescorted men," said one menu notation. "Only good for four hours," advertised another. One guest is said to have placed a sign on his hotel door saying, "Do not disturb; I've just had a Lovers' Salad at Win Schuler's." When asked about the unique taste of the salad—a mixture of greens, bacon, toasted almonds, sliced mushroom caps, and other garnishes with a sweet and sour dressing—Win explained facetiously, "I put my heart into it." ◆ Today, the Lovers' Salad is still available by request, and the restaurant offers a different, but equally "special" enticement before the entree—the "Schuler's Salad," which has a creamy garlic dressing and is available as a side or dinner salad.

Lemon Herb Vinaigrette

2   tablespoons red wine vinegar
    Zest and juice from one lemon
2½ tablespoons minced shallot
    or red onion
2   teaspoons Dijon mustard
1   large garlic clove, minced and mashed
    to a paste with ½ teaspoon of salt
½   teaspoon rounded anchovy paste
1   cup extra-virgin olive oil
1½ teaspoons minced fresh thyme
1½ tablespoons finely chopped fresh basil
    Makes 1½ cups

1   Whisk together vinegar, lemon juice, shallot, mustard, garlic paste, and anchovy paste in a small bowl until combined.

2   Add oil in a slow stream, whisking until emulsified. Whisk in thyme, basil, and salt and pepper to taste.

Sweet and Sour House Dressing

1   cup salad oil
½   cup ketchup
⅓   cup honey
2   tablespoons apple cider vinegar
1   tablespoon fresh lemon juice
2   tablespoons soy sauce
2   tablespoons finely grated onion
2   teaspoons Worcestershire sauce
2   teaspoons salt
    Makes 2½ cups

1   Mix all ingredients well and serve at room temperature. If you refrigerate, the honey and the salad oil will congeal!

Balsamic Vinaigrette

½   cup premium balsamic vinegar
1   cup extra-virgin olive oil
    Salt and fresh ground pepper to taste
    Makes 1½ cups

1   Add the vinegar to a small bowl. Whisk the olive oil into the vinegar in a slow steady stream to blend.

2   Season with salt and pepper to taste. Expect this combination to be strong! Use sparingly or mix the oil and vinegar in a 3 to 1 ratio instead of a 2 to 1, if you prefer.

Bitter Green Salad with Sweet Potatoes, Bacon, and Oranges

I love this dish because it's an unexpected way to use sweet potatoes. For those who have only had sweet potatoes mashed at mom's house on Thanksgiving Day, try this salad for a change of pace. It is easy and delicious. Serve it with a glass of Alsatian Riesling to complete the transformation of this pedestrian spud from an unglamorous side dish to an elegant main attraction.

Bitter Green Salad with Sweet Potatoes, Bacon, and Oranges

½ pound thick cut bacon, sliced thin

2 medium sweet potatoes, cleaned

2 tablespoons olive oil

2 tablespoons fresh orange juice

3 tablespoons soy sauce

4 cloves garlic, crushed

4 oranges, peeled with a knife and sliced across grain

4 ounces Maple Syrup Dressing (pg 38)

1 head frisee and one head radicchio lettuce rinsed and patted dry

Serves 6

1 Preheat oven to 350°.

2 Bake the sweet potatoes for about 20 minutes or until they are about half done. Let them cool slightly, peel off the skins and slice into ¼-inch-thick rounds.

3 While the sweet potatoes are baking, brown the bacon over medium-high heat in a heavy skillet until the bacon is brown and the fat is rendered. Remove the bacon with a slotted spoon and let it drain on paper towels.

4 In a medium bowl combine 2 tablespoons of the bacon fat from the pan, the olive oil, orange juice, soy sauce, and garlic. Whisk to combine, add the potato slices and coat evenly. Set aside to marinate while you start your grill, about 30 minutes.

5 Prepare the Maple Syrup Dressing. Add the potato slices to the grill and cook on both sides until tender throughout. In a large bowl, mix the frisee, radicchio (torn into medium-sized pieces), orange slices, and Maple Syrup Dressing and toss gently to coat. Portion the lettuce mixture onto plates to serve and top with the grilled sweet potatoes and the crispy bacon.

Cantaloupe and Prosciutto with Mixed Greens, Mint, and Mozzarella   {COVER PHOTO}

1 fresh ripe cantaloupe

1 package prosciutto slices

¼ pound mixed baby greens

1 bunch fresh mint leaves

8 ounces fresh mozzarella cheese (or use farmer's cheese as a substitute)

4 ounces Balsamic Vinaigrette (pg 39) Fresh ground pepper to taste

Serves 4

1 Slice the cantaloupe in half, remove the seeds and the rind, and slice it into at least 12 crescent-shaped pieces. Wrap each piece in one of the prosciutto slices. Set aside.

2 Cut the mozzarella into 12 pieces, and set aside. Place a small mound of mixed baby greens onto each of four salad plates. Arrange cantaloupe slices and mozzarella pieces in alternating order on each bed of greens.

3 Toss a few mint leaves over the top, drizzle with the dressing, and grind a bit of black pepper over the plate. Serve the salad with some crusty French bread for some variation in texture.

For those of you who blanch at the idea of eating raw fish, have no fear, this fish isn't actually raw. In technical terms, the acid in the vinegar and the lemon denature (or cook) the proteins in the fish just as a hot flame would. In layman's terms…it's not sushi, and you'll love the taste!

Seviche and Avocado Salad

4   ounces Lemon Herb Vinaigrette (pg 39)
¼   pound salmon filet
¼   pound whitefish filet
¼   pound mixed baby greens
     Sprig fresh dill
1   ripe avocado
6   grape tomatoes
1   tablespoon capers
     Fresh ground black pepper to taste
Serves 2

1 Prepare the Lemon Herb Vinaigrette in a small bowl and set aside. Slice the fish across the grain as thinly as possible.

2 Place the fish in a glass baking dish and pour the vinaigrette over the fish, making sure to coat each piece. Cover and refrigerate for at least one hour. (The longer you soak the fish, the more it will "cook," but you run the risk of turning it mushy.)

3 Remove the pit from the avocado, scoop out the flesh cleanly with a spoon, and cut into attractive crescent slices. Arrange the greens, dill, avocado, and an alternating pattern of salmon and whitefish on two salad plates.

4 Drizzle the extra dressing over the top and garnish with a sprinkle of capers. Serve with Schuler's Whole Wheat Crackers or a chewy French bread. This dish is a superb accompaniment to almost any kind of white wine, light or full-bodied.

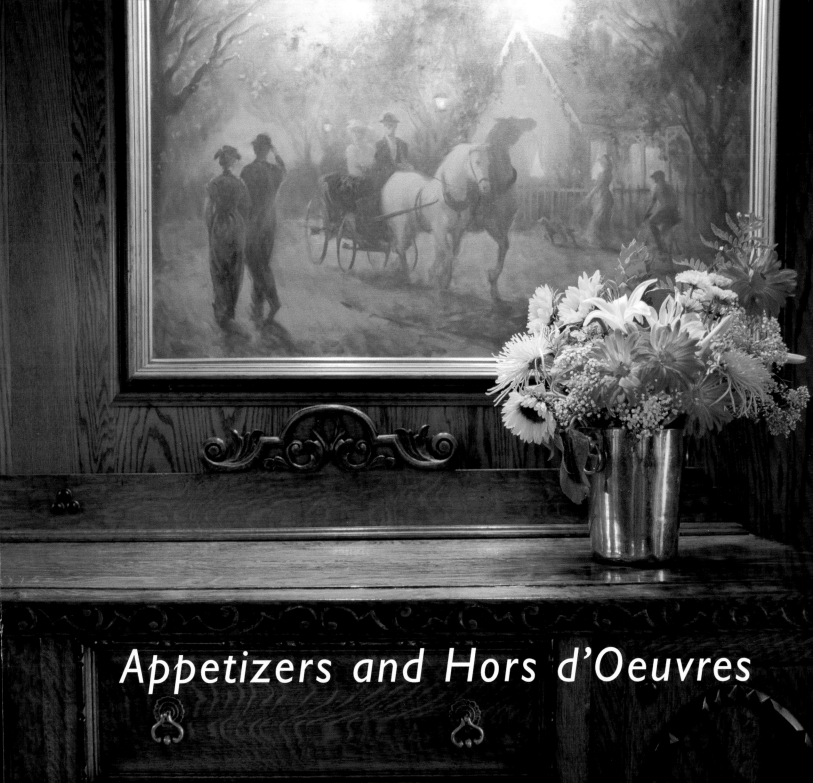

Appetizers and Hors d'Oeuvres

Over the years, Schuler's has consistently featured mushroom caps on its appetizer menu, with subtle changes being stamped upon the original recipe by each new chef that has graced our kitchen. This version has been tampered with yet again by Yours Truly — I think to satisfactory results. One thing is consistent, however. No matter how exactly they are made, people keep ordering and eating them!

Artichoke and Crab Stuffed Mushroom Caps

For mushrooms

20 large (2½ inch diameter) mushrooms. About one pound.

½ teaspoon salt

¼ teaspoon freshly ground pepper

1 tablespoon dry sherry

2 cloves crushed garlic

1 tablespoon olive oil

For filling

2 tablespoons olive oil

Mushroom stems, finely chopped in food processor

1 medium onion, finely chopped

¼ cup celery, finely chopped

2 garlic cloves, finely chopped

2 ounces cream cheese

3 slices firm white bread, finely chopped in food processor

1 teaspoon Creole Seasoning (pg 26)

½ teaspoon fresh oregano, finely chopped

1 ounces finely grated Parmesan cheese

1 10-ounce can lump crabmeat, chopped and drained

1 10-ounce can artichoke hearts, chopped and drained

¼ cup fresh parsley, finely chopped

2 tablespoons unsalted butter, melted

Serves 6–8

1 Preheat oven to 400°. Remove the stems from the mushrooms and set them aside for filling. Make sure the caps are clean. If not, wipe them off with a clean, wet towel.

2 In a large bowl, mix the sherry, oil, garlic, salt and pepper and toss with the mushrooms until the caps are coated.

3 Bake the caps, upside down, for 10–15 minutes or until the caps start to give off liquid. Remove from the oven.

4 Heat the olive oil in a large Dutch oven over medium-high heat. Add the mushrooms, onion, celery, and garlic and sauté until tender.

5 Turn the heat to low and add the cream cheese until soft and incorporated with the vegetables. Then add the rest of the ingredients and stir with a heavy spoon until combined.

6 Turn the caps over and stuff generously with the filling—mounded the higher, the better. Return to the oven and bake for another 20 minutes until the mushrooms are tender and the stuffing is golden brown.

7 Garnish with an additional sprinkle of parsley and Parmesan cheese.

One of the characteristics of a Schuler meatball is that it is tender, not chewy or crispy. To achieve this end, make sure to use fresh breadcrumbs. A couple of slices of tender white bread in the food processor should do the trick.

Schuler's Famous Meatballs

1   cup fresh bread crumbs
1½   cup milk
2   medium onions
2½   pounds ground round
1½   pounds ground pork
1   large egg
2½   teaspoons salt
¾   teaspoon freshly ground black pepper
¼   cup minced fresh flat-leafed parsley leaves
Makes about 3 dozen meatballs

1 In a large bowl soak the breadcrumbs in milk for 10 minutes. Finely chop the onion. Add the onion and remaining meatball ingredients to the breadcrumb mixture and blend together by hand until combined.

2 Form the mixture into walnut-size balls and arrange on large trays or baking sheets.

3 Balls can be fried until brown in about ½ cup olive oil in a heavy skillet. Or, if you want to save a step and the mess of frying, place the sheet pans in the oven at 350° and bake until brown.

4 To finish the meatballs, place in a Dutch oven and cover with Schuler's Barbecue Sauce. Heat over a medium-low flame until the sauce and meatballs are heated throughout.

If you walk into Schuler's kitchen today, this is the recipe they follow to make up the spread that is offered with the Whole Wheat Crackers and bread selection at the restaurant. Add more or less of any of these ingredients to suit your taste buds and call the spread your own!

Schuler's Heritage Cheese Spread

4   ounces sharp cheddar cheese
8   ounces garbanzo beans
8   ounces cream cheese
5   ounces sour cream
1   tablespoon white vinegar
2   teaspoons salt
1   tablespoon sugar
1   tablespoon paprika
¼   cup unsalted butter
½   cup mayonnaise
¼   cup buttermilk
1   ounce prepared horseradish
    Dash of brown ale
Serves 8–12

1 Start by grinding the cheddar cheese and then the garbanzo beans in a food processor. Transfer the ingredients to a mixer with a paddle attachment.

2 Add the cream cheese, sour cream, and butter and beat until smooth. Then simply add the rest of the ingredients and beat until the cheese has a well-mixed and spreadable consistency.

So good, so simple. Put out a crock of this with crusty French bread or Whole Wheat Crackers and prepare to please your friends who love bold flavors. For an exciting change of pace, put a dollop on Roasted Beets or the Roasted Vegetable Panini.

Goat Cheese Gratin

8   ounces packet Montrachet or other soft goat cheese
4   ounces cream cheese
¼   cup heavy whipping cream
¼   cup freshly grated Parmesan cheese
½   teaspoon finely chopped fresh tarragon
¼   teaspoon kosher salt
    Freshly ground black pepper to taste
    Serves 8

1   Combine the ingredients in a double boiler and stir over medium-low heat until the contents are warm and bubbly. Serve hot in ramekins or crocks convenient for dipping, or spoon liberal amounts onto the bread or cracker of your choice.

Prosciutto Cheese Straws

1   sheet puff pastry
    Egg wash, made of 1 egg and 2 teaspoons water
4   ounces sharp cheddar cheese, shredded fine
¼   teaspoon cayenne pepper
4   ounces prosciutto ham slices
    Kosher salt to taste
    Serves 4

1   Preheat the oven to 425°. Roll out puff pastry sheet on a lightly floured surface into a 12" by 14" rectangle and brush with some egg wash.

2   Cut in half lengthways and sprinkle cheese, ham, and cayenne pepper on one half. Lay the other half, egg wash down, on top, and gently roll out to eliminate air pockets. Brush again with egg wash and sprinkle with salt. Cut the pastry lengthways into ½-inch-wide strips.

3   Twist the strips and put them on a lined baking sheet to bake. Pinch the ends to keep the straws from coming apart. Bake for 10–12 minutes or until golden brown.

Don't be intimidated by this raw beef dish. Simply make sure that the beef you use is fresh from the butcher and well trimmed of its outer layering of silver skin. This salad is terrific with hearty French bread, which can be used to sop up the dressing and to nudge the tasty bits of beef and peppery arugula onto your fork. Hunters should try this recipe with venison loin—the effect is even more spectacular.

Beef Carpaccio and Arugula with Lemon Herb Vinaigrette

¾ pound trimmed beef fillet
(cut from the thick end)

1 cup thinly sliced arugula, washed
well and patted dry with a clean cloth

½ cup Parmesan curls (made by
shaving a wedge of Parmesan
with a vegetable peeler)

½ cup Lemon Herb Vinaigrette Dressing
(pg 39)

Freshly ground black pepper to taste

Serves 4

1 Freeze the beef, wrapped in a plastic wrap, for 1 hour, or until it is firm but not frozen solid. With a very sharp knife, cut the beef across the grain into ⅛-inch-thick slices.

2 Arrange the slices about 3 inches apart on sheets of plastic wrap. Cover them with additional sheets of wrap, and with a rolling pin, roll the slices thin, testing the first rolled slice to make sure it is not too thin to be lifted from the plastic without tearing. Loosely roll up the sheets of plastic and chill the beef for at least 1 hour (up to 3 hours).

3 Divide the beef slices among 4 chilled plates. Serve with the arugula alone or combine with fresh herbs and vegetables. Crack fresh pepper over the top and drizzle with the vinaigrette.

The taste of this dish seems to have a universal appeal. I have a friend who is the proverbial picky eater, but who loves shrimp prepared this way. Give it a whirl and watch your discriminating friends clean their plates, too.

Potted Shrimp

1 stick butter, softened

1 tablespoon lemon juice

2 tablespoons sherry

Pinch of Creole Seasoning (pg 26)

½ pound small (less expensive)
shrimp, peeled, cooked, and chopped

4 ounces cream cheese, softened

5 tablespoons chives, finely chopped

Serves 4

1 Combine all ingredients in a small bowl and stir with a wooden spatula until well mixed. Mound in a small crock and let everything chill for an hour before serving. This dish is great with crackers, toast points, or any other kind of bread with a crunchy consistency.

I hated liver until my dad convinced me to try a house pâté at a wonderful French restaurant in Toronto.
(No, I was twelve; I can't remember the name of the restaurant!) Much to my surprise it was terrific! Ever since,
I have been slathering foie gras on crusty bread and crackers every chance I get. I concocted this version to
utilize the venison liver that always seems to be in large supply around our family farm. Put this out on the
hors d'oeuvres table for the holidays with some port wine and transport your family back to a more elegant time.
Served in front of a roaring fire, it's particularly certain to please.

Pâté du Maison with a Rhubarb Port Wine Reduction

For pâté

1	small bread loaf pan
1/2	pound thick-cut bacon, whole
3	strips thick-cut bacon, finely diced
1	medium onion, finely chopped
1/2	pound venison liver, skinned and trimmed
1/2	pound chicken liver, cleaned and trimmed
1/2	cup cognac
1/4	cup good quality mayonnaise
2	tablespoons heavy whipping cream
1	teaspoon dried thyme
1 1/2	teaspoons kosher salt
	Freshly ground black pepper
1	teaspoon crushed juniper berries
1/2	teaspoon allspice
1/2	cup walnuts
3	tablespoons chopped fresh parsley

For sauce

4	medium-sized stalks of rhubarb, cleaned and finely diced
1/2	cup sugar
	Pinch of salt
1 1/2	cups port wine

Serves 10–12

1 Preheat oven to 300°. Prepare the pan by placing the whole bacon across the bottom of the pan with the ends climbing the sides and hanging over the edges. (The loose ends will be folded over the pâté immediately before putting it in the oven.) Leave no spot uncovered.

2 Sauté the diced bacon in a large skillet until the fat is rendered and add the onion, venison liver, and chicken liver. Most of the cooking will be done in the oven, but this is a good time to tenderize the onion and brown the liver on the outside.

3 When the liver turns brown, add the cognac (be careful to pull the pan away from the stove when adding the alcohol) and cook until the flame subsides. Add the contents of the pan to a blender, making sure to scrape all the brown bits off of the bottom of the pan (for extra flavor).

4 Add the mayonnaise and cream and process until smooth. Add the thyme, salt, pepper, juniper berries, and allspice, and blend the mixture again. Finally, throw in the chopped walnuts and parsley and pulse until barely blended.

5 Pour the mixture into the bacon-covered pan and fold over the top bacon ends to make a sealed envelope. Place the pan in a larger pan. Fill the larger pan with hot water halfway up the sides on the smaller pâté pan (called a Bain Marie) and bake in the oven until the pâté loaf starts to pull away from the sides and a toothpick poked into the center comes out dry. Remove from the oven and let the small pan cool in the fridge for several hours before serving.

6 In one saucepan, heat the rhubarb with the sugar and pinch of salt over medium heat, stirring regularly. In another, heat the port wine over high heat. When the rhubarb starts to look like a stringy applesauce and the port wine has been reduced by half, combine the two pots and you'll have a sauce. Cool before serving.

Schuler's makes three-quarters of a million of these crackers each year!

House-Made Whole Wheat Crackers

2   cups crushed wheat flour
7   cups bread flour
1   tablespoon salt
1   teaspoon extra-active yeast
3   cups water
1½ tablespoon honey
¾   cup olive oil
    Serves 8

1   Mix the dough as you would any normal dough. Mix the dry ingredients together. Add honey, oil, and ¾ cups of water. Using the dough hook on a mixer, knead the dough and water until you have smooth dough that stretches well. Let the dough rest ½–1 hour.

2   Roll out onto large floured surface until roughly the size of a full sheet pan or about ⅛ inch thick. Top with olive oil and the following ingredients:

    1 teaspoon granulated garlic
    4 teaspoons table salt
    1 teaspoon kosher salt

3   Cut into 1 to 2 inch strips and put on two baking sheets. Bake at 440° with steam for 15 minutes. (Spray water on the inside walls of the oven before you shut the door.)

Grilled Sourdough Toast Points

4   thick slices sourdough bread
    Olive oil for brushing
    Serves 4

1   Brush slices of the sourdough bread with olive oil, and cook on a hot grill until the bread is brown and scored black on both sides. Be patient, as the black grill marks impart much of the flavor. Cut diagonally into toast points and serve hot in a covered basket.

Garlic Crostini Chips

1   baguette or similar long, French-style loaf
    Olive oil for brushing
4   cloves garlic, crushed
    Serves 4

1   Preheat the oven to 425°.

2   Cut the baguette on an angle into ¼-inch-thick disks. Combine the crushed garlic with the olive oil and brush on both sides of the bread.

3   Place on a lined sheet pan and bake in the oven until the crostinis are golden brown. Serve in a covered breadbasket to keep warm.

Herbed Focaccia

For sponge

1¾ cup bread flour

1 cup water

¼ teaspoon instant yeast

For final dough

3¾ cups bread flour

½ to 1 cup water

¼ teaspoon instant yeast

1 tablespoon salt

3 tablespoons olive oil

For herbed oil

1 cup olive oil

1 tablespoon dried oregano

1 tablespoon dried basil

Simmer 10 minutes on medium heat and let cool.

Makes 8 large sandwich loaves

Sponge

1 Stir the ingredients together to form a smooth thick batter. Cover and leave out overnight.

Dough

2 Mix the ingredients by hand or by using a dough hook on your mixer (the amount of water needed may vary, so start with about half a cup and go from there). Add the sponge. Knead the dough until it is smooth and stretchy. Place the dough in a bowl, cover it with plastic, and leave it in a warm spot for half an hour.

3 Then turn out the dough on a floured board, press and fold it over twice, and return it to the bowl for another half hour. Place the dough onto the floured board and divide it into 8–10 evenly shaped pieces. Round the pieces as you would a ball of playdough. Place the balls on the floured board and let them rest for 20 minutes.

4 Preheat oven to 425°.

5 With the palm of your hand, press the pieces of dough out to approximately 4 inches in diameter. Place the dough on a sheet pan that has been greased and covered with cornmeal. Brush the focaccia with herbed oil and let it rise until it has doubled in size. Just before you bake the focaccia, use your finger to make small indentations on top of the dough. Just after you place the dough into the oven, spray water onto the inner sides of the oven to produce steam and then close the oven. Bake for 20 minutes or until brown. Place on a rack to cool.

not leave a better legacy to than an educated family.

— Harry S Truman

This is a great dish to put out on an hors d'oeuvres buffet at a cocktail party. It's attractive and tasty enough to make your guests want to return for more. It's also substantial enough to keep people from starving while they sample your selections from the bar. The dish is a bit heavy to serve before a dinner party, unless you are entertaining some "big eaters."

Savory Pesto Cheesecake

For crust

1¾ cups fresh bread crumbs from French bread

1 cup freshly grated Parmesan cheese (about 3 ounces)

6 tablespoons (¾ stick) butter, melted

For pesto

4 cups packed fresh basil leaves, washed well

½ cup pine nuts, toasted until golden, cooled, and finely chopped

½ cup freshly grated Parmesan (about 1½ ounces)

2 large garlic cloves, minced

¼ cup extra-virgin olive oil

1 small jar sun-dried tomatoes (for garnish)

For filling

1 tablespoon olive oil

1 cup chopped onion

1 cup chopped red bell pepper

4 cups coarsely chopped assorted fresh wild mushrooms (such as crimini, oyster and stemmed shiitake)

3 8-ounce packages cream cheese, room temperature

2 teaspoons salt

1 teaspoon ground black pepper

4 large eggs

½ cup whipping cream

½ cup grated Parmesan cheese

1 cup grated Gruyère cheese

½ cup chopped fresh parsley

Crust

1 Preheat oven to 350°. Mix all ingredients in medium bowl until well blended. Press mixture onto the bottom (not the sides) of a 9-inch-diameter springform pan with 2¾-inch high sides. Bake crust until golden brown, about 12 minutes. Cool the crust while preparing the filling. Maintain oven temperature.

Pesto

2 In a food processor, puree basil with remaining ingredients until smooth, and season with salt and pepper.

Filling

3 Heat 1 tablespoon of oil in a heavy large skillet over medium-high heat. Add chopped onion and bell pepper and sauté 2 minutes. Add the mushrooms and sauté until the liquid evaporates and mushrooms begin to brown, about 10 minutes. Cool.

4 Using an electric mixer, beat the cream cheese with salt and pepper in a large bowl until fluffy. Beat in the eggs one at a time, followed by the whipping cream. With a spatula, fold in the vegetable mixture, Parmesan, Gruyère, and chopped parsley.

5 Pour half of the filling over the crust, and then spoon half of the pesto mixture over the top, evenly spreading the pesto with the back of the spoon. Pour the remaining filling over the pesto layer and put the cheesecake on a baking sheet. Bake until the cake puffs and browns on the top, but the center still moves slightly when the pan is shaken, about 1 hour and 15 minutes. Transfer the cake to a rack and cool.

6 To serve, run a sharp knife around the pan to loosen the cake and release the springform pan. Place on a serving platter and top with the remaining pesto and some sun-dried tomato slices. Serve with Garlic Crostini Chips or House-made Whole Wheat Crackers (pg 52).

I use precooked and marinated artichoke hearts for this dish, because it is so much easier.
Serve as a side dish or as an appetizer.

Baked Artichoke Hearts with Bread Crumbs and Fresh Herbs {PHOTO PG 6}

12 baby artichoke hearts, stems removed
¼   cup extra-virgin olive oil
1   cup fresh bread crumbs
¼   cup grated Parmesan cheese
1½ teaspoon herbes de Provence
    Salt and pepper to taste,
1   tablespoon chopped fresh herbs
    (lavender and thyme, to suggest two)
    Serves 2–4

1 Preheat the oven to 350°.

2 Arrange the baby artichokes in a honeycomb pattern in a shallow baking dish. In a small bowl, mix the olive oil, bread crumbs, Parmesan cheese, herbes de Provence, salt and pepper. Spoon the mixture over the artichokes and sprinkle with the chopped herbs.

3 Bake until the artichokes are hot and the bread crumbs are beginning to brown, about 15 minutes. Serve with Grilled Sourdough Toast Points (pg 52).

Tapenade is like Provençale caviar. Once you fall in love with the taste, you won't be able to get enough.

Tapenade Stuffed Cherry Tomatoes

1   pint ripe cherry tomatoes,
    tops cut off and seeds scooped out
1   cup pitted black olives, salt cured
½   cup anchovy filets
½   cup capers
¼   cup extra-virgin olive oil
    Salt and pepper to taste
    Serves 6

1 Mash the olives with the anchovies and the capers with a mortar and pestle. Add the olive oil until the mixture is creamy and stir in a small amount of salt and pepper.

2 Spoon the mixture into the individual tomato cups and put out on an hors d'oeuvres buffet or pass with cocktails. The flavor will nearly explode in your mouth!

It's not how much but how

— W. J. Schuler

In Michigan, many of us eagerly await the first morel hunt of the spring. For people who love food, this is akin to "trick or treating" on Halloween. The primary difference is that our pillowcases are filled with delicious mushrooms, rather than candy. This recipe makes sure that these little treats never go to waste.

Creamy Sautéed Morel Mushrooms

1 tablespoon clarified butter

1 big handful of morel mushrooms, brushed of any sediment, dirt, or debris

1 tablespoon finely diced onion

1 garlic clove, crushed

1 tablespoon white wine

¼ cup heavy whipping cream

2 tablespoons fresh bread crumbs

1 teaspoon fresh chopped parsley and rosemary

Salt and pepper to taste

1 Heat a large skillet over medium heat and coat with the clarified butter. Add the mushrooms, being careful not to crowd the pan too much, and let them cook until brown.

2 Add the onions and garlic and cook a minute more until the onions and garlic soften. Add the white wine to loosen the bits of onion and garlic on the bottom of the pan, then add the cream and start to reduce. To thicken, add the bread crumbs and toss in the herbs for added flavor. Salt and pepper to taste.

3 Garnish with Parmesan cheese if you prefer. This mixture is good as a stand-alone dish, stuffed in a nice trout, or served over toast with a side salad. Great with a buttery, oaky Chardonnay!

Pan-Fried Oysters with Spicy Remoulade Sauce

24 shucked oysters, drained

2 cups yellow cornmeal

1 teaspoon freshly ground black pepper

1 teaspoon cayenne pepper

Vegetable oil for pan frying

4 ounces Spicy Remoulade Sauce (pg 30)

Serves 4

1 Mix together the cornmeal, black pepper, and cayenne pepper in a heavy-duty plastic bag.

2 Working in batches of six, place the oysters in the bag and shake to coat, making sure to knock off any excess cornmeal as you remove the oysters from the bag. In a heavy kettle or cast iron skillet, heat 1½ inches of the vegetable oil to 375° (turn the stove to medium and wait for the oil to start roiling in the pan).

3 Fry the oysters in batches of six until golden and barely cooked through… about 1½ minutes. (Flip once to fry both sides.) Transfer the oysters with a slotted spoon to paper towels to drain.

4 Serve with lemon wedges and a ramekin of Remoulade sauce for dipping. As an alternative, serve on warm French bread, halved and buttered, with sauce, a squeeze of lemon and some shredded lettuce for an Oyster Po' Boy. Ripe tomatoes are optional, but recommended.

, This is my mom's corn bread recipe with jalapeño thrown in for good measure.
I always make a pan when fixing Michigan Bean Soup, Barbecued Baby Back Ribs, or a good pot of chili.

Jalapeño Corn Bread

1   box Jiffy corn bread mix
1   can cream corn (4 ounce)
¼   cup sour cream
1   egg
1–2 jalapeños, seeded and chopped fine
   Serves 8–12

1 Preheat oven to 350°.

2 De-seed and chop the jalapeños with gloves on, so your fingers won't be burned by the chilies. In a small bowl, mix together all the ingredients and pour them into an 8-inch-square greased casserole pan. Bake for 35 minutes or until firm and golden, not crumbly.

Sandwiches

A restaurant or deli's fancy panini maker is like a George Foreman grill, only bigger.
Try this on your home grill or, if you don't have one, use a heavy skillet and cook the
sandwich like a grilled cheese. Either way, you'll be pleased with the results.

Roasted Vegetable Panini with Handmade Hummus and Feta Cheese

For hummus

2   garlic cloves, crushed

½   teaspoon salt

1   16-ounce can chickpeas, rinsed
    and drained

⅓   cup tahini (sesame seed paste)

1   teaspoon ground cumin

2   tablespoons fresh lemon juice

2   tablespoons olive oil

3   tablespoons water

3   tablespoons minced fresh parsley leaves

For panini

2   zucchini, sliced lengthways

1   eggplant, sliced lengthways

1   onion, sliced

1   green pepper, sliced

1   red pepper, sliced

1   portabella mushroom, sliced

¼   cup olive oil

    Kosher salt and fresh ground pepper

4   ounces crumbled feta cheese

8   large slices hearty white bread,
    like a French loaf or a sourdough

    Olive oil spray for grilling

1   Preheat the oven to 400°.

2   To make the hummus, combine the garlic, salt, chickpeas, tahini, and cumin in the food processor until well blended. While the processor is still running, pour in the lemon juice, olive oil, and water. Add the parsley and pulse until combined.

3   In a large bowl, combine the zucchini, eggplant, onion, peppers, and mushroom with the olive oil and salt and pepper. Transfer to the roasting pan and cook until the vegetables are tender and turning brown, about 30 minutes.

4   When the vegetables are done, divide them up on four slices of the bread and cover with feta cheese. On another four slices, spread some of the hummus and put the two sides together to make a sandwich.

5   Spray the sandwiches with olive oil and heat through on your panini grill or cook until golden brown on both sides in a heavy skillet. Serve with potato chips and ice-cold beer.

This is my version of a Cuban sandwich with my mother's famous Hot Mustard Sauce
to really give it an extra boost. If your have ever wondered what to do with leftovers
from a pork roast, here is your chance to do something memorable.

Ham and Roast Pork Panini with Pickle and Hot Mustard

1 loaf French bread
2 ounces Hot Mustard Sauce (pg 28)
12 ounces ham
12 ounces cold roasted pork, thinly sliced
8 ounces Swiss cheese
10 dill pickle slices
2 ounces mayonnaise
2 tablespoons butter
Serves 4

1 Split the loaf in two, lengthways. Slather the bottom half with the hot mustard and stack with the ham, pork, Swiss cheese, and pickles. Spread the mayonnaise on the other half and close the sandwich.

2 Cut the loaf into four equal lengths. Butter the outside of the bread and toast the sandwiches in a medium-hot skillet or on a panini grill until the outside is toasty brown and the cheese is melted on the inside.

Schuler's Classic Reuben Sandwich

2 slices hearty light rye bread
5 ounces top quality corned beef brisket
2 thick slices Swiss or Gruyère cheese
2 ounces canned or fresh sauerkraut, rinsed
2 tablespoons Thousand Island dressing
1 tablespoon butter, softened
Serves 1

1 Heat a cast iron skillet over medium heat and mix the sauerkraut in a bowl with the Thousand Island dressing.

2 On the bottom slice of rye, stack the cheese and then the corned beef. Spread the sauerkraut dressing mixture evenly over the beef and top with the second slice of bread. Butter both sides of the sandwich before placing it in the skillet.

3 Cook until golden brown on bottom, then flip and repeat. You may want to cover the skillet while browning the sandwich to help the cheese melt. This is made to be enjoyed with your favorite beer. Schuler's Brew, perhaps?

When he saw that the bar was no longer producing much in the way of business for the restaurant, Hans Schuler introduced the pub concept in the early 1980s. When others might have basked in the reputation and success of the flagship restaurant, he saw an opportunity in the changing eating habits of the public. Reasoning that many people would come in to get "an exceptional hamburg and a mug of beer," Hans set about to create a "second restaurant" adjacent to the existing Centennial Room. A grill was put in, and Hans aggressively went after the local customers who might use the pub as a meeting place or for a more casual meal. Win Schuler had his doubts. "What, are you going to have another McDonalds here?" he asked Hans. The Pub would prove to be a popular mid-week gathering place, however, and Win would later enthusiastically embrace the results of his son's vision. Today, the Pub carries Win's name. ◆ Like its namesake, Winston's Pub values personal interaction. To facilitate a regular exchange of ideas and to further promote loyalty, in the mid-1990s Hans Schuler formed a group of more than 30 area customers into a "Pub Advisory Board" that meets several times a year to review new menu items, provide feedback, and participate in promotional activities. "It's a great

A Hamburg and a Stein of Beer: Winston's Pub

way for 'regulars' to be recognized and for useful suggestions to be solicited," says John Brundage, a charter member of the board. "Hans particularly values the opinions of his longtime, local customers, and the Advisory Board was his brainchild. We do have a lot of fun, and it gives the restaurant a valuable focus group." ◆ During the past decade, a $1.4 million renovation of the restaurant included an expansion of the Pub, and the installation of a separate kitchen to facilitate pub dining. By sponsoring events such as "Celebrity Bartender Night" and musical entertainment, the Pub adds to the camaraderie of the local casual dining scene.

John Brundage enjoys a glass of Chardonnay with the assistance of bartender Darin Lee.

This is not a sandwich you make for yourself, unless you have leftover beef brisket.
This is the type of sandwich you make for a pack of hungry football fans coming
over to watch the game. Just make sure you serve a bottomless bowl of chips, too.

Hot Beef Brisket Sandwich with Smoked Gouda on Grilled Sourdough

I   beef brisket, trimmed
I   tablespoon Schuler's Seasoning Salt (pg 30)
I   tablespoon fennel
I   loaf hearty sourdough bread
½   pound smoked Gouda cheese
6   ounces Garlic and Herb Aioli (pg 30)
4   ounces butter, softened
   Serves 8

1 Preheat the oven to 350°.

2 Pat the brisket down with Seasoning Salt and fennel and place it in a roasting pan. Put the brisket in the oven, uncovered, and bake until fork tender. This could take as long as three hours, depending on the cut of the meat. If the brisket is getting too brown, cover the pan until the meat is done.

3 Heat a large heavy skillet over medium heat. After the meat has cooled slightly, cut across the grain into ½-inch-thick slices. Lay out half of your bread slices and cover them with the Gouda cheese. Divide up the beef over the cheese, leaving a good heaping on each slice. Put a dollop of the aioli on the slices to cover the sandwiches. Finally, butter each sandwich and start browning them in the pan. You will probably have to do these in batches. The inside will be hot from the beef, so the cheese will melt easily. The goal should be to get the outside crispy and golden. Serve immediately.

Find the best of each of these ingredients, and this sandwich will be a special treat.
Good, ripe tomatoes are an excellent start, along with high quality bacon.
Brie can be substituted for Camembert with equally desirable results.

Fresh Basil, Tomato, and Camembert on Grilled Sourdough

1   teaspoon olive oil
2   slices hearty sourdough bread
4   strips thick-cut bacon
3   ounces Camembert cheese, room temperature
3   large leaves basil
3   slices vine ripened tomatoes
1   teaspoon Garlic and Herb Aioli (pg 30)
Serves 1

1   Preheat the grill.

2   Cook the bacon in either a skillet or the oven (350° in the oven works great if you haven't tried it before), about 20 minutes.

3   Brush the outside of the sourdough with the olive oil and place it on the grill. (A skillet works in a pinch, but the flavor from the grill helps make this sandwich special.) Cook until the bread is browned and you see the telltale black hatch marks.

4   Remove the bread from the grill and sandwich the Camembert, basil, tomato slices, bacon, and garlic aioli between the slices. Then see if you can make it to the table. I've been known to jump the gun and eat this over the sink!

Tired of tuna fish sandwiches? Well, this ought to help. My attitude is that anything that is fantastic on its own can only be better surrounded by bread and covered in sauce. I love tuna grilled rare, and a tuna hero is my idea of heaven!

Mediterranean-Style Grilled Tuna Steak Hero

I tuna steak, 4–6 ounces, grilled (leftovers work well, too)

a few sprigs fresh herbs (dill, a must—oregano, tarragon, and Italian parsley also are delicious)

small handful mixed baby greens

I hard-boiled egg, sliced

½ cup cure pitted black olives, chopped

I ounce Garlic and Herb Aioli (pg 30)

I ounce marinara sauce

I small loaf whole wheat baguette

Serves I

I If possible, find a chewy, crunchy, whole-wheat French baguette (yes, they exist). Split the baguette in half and cover one half with the garlic aioli and the other with the marinara sauce. Balance the grilled tuna, fresh herbs, mixed baby greens, hard-boiled eggs, and black olives between the bread and attempt to eat. The result is likely to be messy, juicy…and delicious.

The recipe for focaccia in this book is an excellent one and is worth the trouble, but focaccia from the grocery also works well. The peppery flavor of the arugula with the savory chicken and the garlic in the aioli are what make this sandwich special.

Chicken and Arugula Sandwich on Focaccia

I	loaf focaccia bread
I	six-ounce chicken breast
I	tablespoon fresh squeezed lemon juice
I	tablespoon olive oil
I	clove garlic, crushed
	Salt and pepper to taste
I	tablespoon Garlic and Herb Aioli (pg 30)
½	cup fresh arugula
2	thin slices red onion

Serves I

1 First, marinate the chicken by combining the lemon, olive oil, garlic, salt, and pepper in a nonreactive bowl and pouring the mixture into a freezer bag with the chicken. Refrigerate for at least a couple of hours (or a day or two if you like). When you are ready to make the sandwich, you can pan-fry it in a hot skillet or throw it on the grill if you prefer. Make sure the chicken is done, but still tender.

2 To assemble the sandwich, lay open the focaccia and cover the insides with the garlic aioli. Fill with chicken breast, red onion, and arugula, and fold together.

In our house, the day-after-Christmas prime rib sandwich is even more revered than the day-after-Thanksgiving turkey sandwich. This holiday season make sure that you have some good blue cheese in the house, create some onion relish, and be ready to make the 26th a celebration, too.

Prime Rib Sandwich with Sweet Onion Relish and Maytag Blue Cheese

6–8	ounces prime rib (leftover and reheated or fresh out of the oven)
2	ounces Maytag blue cheese
2	ounces sweet onion relish
I	tablespoon Horseradish Cream Sauce (pg 27)
I	slice rye bread, toasted

Serves I

1 Toast the rye bread, lay down the warmed prime rib, dollop it with the onion relish, and sprinkle with blue cheese. Serve horseradish sauce on the side so you can dip your knife in it for more sauce as you cut into your sandwich. The nap following this treat is optional (as is the jog, followed by another sandwich!)

Chicken and Arugula Sandwich on Focaccia

When I make these at work I slow-roast an entire top round of beef, which weighs about 23 pounds trimmed, and then I slice it thin on a mechanical slicer. Unless you plan on preparing this recipe for about 40 of your closest friends, you might want to ask your butcher for a smaller cut or use some leftover prime rib that you have reheated. Don't buy precooked roast beef from the deli case, however; it really won't approach the quality of beef that you can roast yourself.

French Dip with Gruyère Cheese

1   small beef roast, trimmed
1   ounce Schuler's Seasoning Salt (pg 30)
1   onion, quartered
1   carrot, quartered
1   stalk celery, quartered
2   cups beef stock, or canned low-sodium beef broth
½   pound Gruyère cheese
    Enough French or Italian bread to make four good-sized sandwiches.

Serves 4

1   Preheat the oven to 300°.

2   Sprinkle the roast with the Seasoning Salt and place the meat on top of the vegetables in a roasting pan. Roast the beef in the oven until the internal temperature reaches 135°. This could take from 45 minutes to two hours, depending on the size of your roast and your oven. Remove and let the meat rest while you make the au jus.

3   To make the au jus, discard the vegetables from the pan and pour off the excess fat. Return the pan to the top of the stove and pour in the beef stock. While heating up the stock in the pan, scrape the bottom of the pan to get all those little bits of flavor into the au jus. Keep everything hot until you serve.

4   To assemble the sandwiches, heat the bread in the oven until crispy on the outside. Then slice the beef as thin as possible across the grain, and stack on the bread with the Gruyère cheese. Serve with a soup cup of the au jus for dipping. Put a little garlic aioli on the side if that interests you and serve the sandwiches with potato chips or fries.

Soup and Stews

Schuler's Swiss Onion Soup

Schuler's Swiss Onion Soup

½ cup butter

2 pounds onions, thinly sliced

1½ teaspoons Hungarian paprika

6 cups beef stock or low-sodium canned beef broth

½ cup vegetable oil

½ cup flour

¾ teaspoon celery salt

Salt and pepper to taste

8 ounces dark beer

12 slices French bread

12 slices Gruyère cheese

Parmesan cheese, grated

Serves 12

1 Cook the onions with the butter in a small stockpot over medium-high heat until the onions are brown but not burned. This will take about 30 minutes. Stir regularly. Sprinkle in the paprika, then add the beef stock and bring to a boil.

2 Make a roux at the same time you are browning the onions by whisking the oil and flour together in a saucepan over medium heat. Watch carefully and stir consistently so as not to burn the roux. It will develop a popcorn smell first and then slowly turn brown. (You want a rich brown color for this recipe.) Stir the roux into the soup when done and add the celery salt. Simmer for at least two hours.

3 Shortly before serving, sprinkle the slices of bread with Parmesan cheese and toast them in the oven. Add the beer and allow the soup to return to serving temperature. Remove from heat.

4 Ladle the soup into individual bowls or serving crocks, top with toasted bread and place a slice of Gruyère cheese over the top of each bowl. Place under the broiler for just a bit, watching carefully, until the cheese is melted, bubbly, and slightly brown.

This is a fresh version that you can make during corn season. If it's January and you don't have any corn from the summer harvest in the freezer, go ahead and use creamed corn as a substitute for the corn and heavy cream in this recipe.

Midwestern Corn Chowder

6 ears of fresh corn, shucked

2 cups heavy cream

1 red bell pepper, diced fine

¼ pound slab bacon cut into thin strips

1 onion, peeled and finely diced

1 garlic clove

4 celery stalks

4 russet potatoes, peeled and diced

1 sprig fresh tarragon

Chopped fresh chives

Serves 4–6

1 Cut the kernels from the ears of corn with a sharp knife and reserve. Steep the cobs in the cream in a saucepan over low heat for about 10 minutes. Turn off the heat and let the mixture sit until you are ready for the cream. In a heavy pot, cook the bacon over medium-low heat until the fat is rendered and the bacon is brown. Remove the bacon with a slotted spoon and set it aside.

2 Add the red pepper, onion, garlic, and celery and cook the mixture in the bacon fat until the vegetables are tender. Add the potatoes and cook them for a few more minutes or until they start to soften. Stir in the reserved corn. Finally, stir in the chicken stock, tarragon, and strained cream (cobs removed) and simmer the chowder until the potatoes are tender, about 20 minutes more. Serve garnished with the chives and bacon bits.

Schuler's Seafood Chowder

¼   cup butter
¼   cup flour
1   small onion, diced
3   stalks celery, diced
6   strips bacon, diced
     Pinch nutmeg
     Pinch cumin
½   teaspoon celery seed
     Dash white pepper
     Dash dried or fresh thyme
     Dash cayenne pepper
2   cloves garlic, crushed
1   cup clam juice
1   cup chicken stock
1   tablespoon lemon juice
1   tablespoon Worcestershire sauce
1   cup white wine
1   cup heavy whipping cream
1   cup diced potatoes
½   cup chopped clams
½   cup rock shrimp
½   cup scallops
½   cup crabmeat
1   cup frozen corn
1   red pepper, diced
     Salt and pepper
1   tablespoon chopped parsley
Serves 8

1 In a small saucepan, start your roux over medium-low heat by combining the butter and flour and whisking until the mixture looks blond and begins to smell like popcorn. This should take about 10 minutes.

2 In a large heavy pot, cook the onion, celery, bacon, spices, and garlic until the onion's liquid starts to release. Add the clam juice, chicken stock, lemon juice, Worcestershire, wine, heavy cream, and potatoes. Simmer for about 20 minutes or until the potatoes are tender.

3 Thicken the chowder by stirring in the roux with your whisk. Finally, add the clams, shrimp, scallops, crabmeat, corn, and red pepper and heat through. Salt and pepper to taste. Serve with a dollop of whipped cream and some extra seafood on the top. Sprinkle with fresh chopped parsley.

My good friend Chef Bill Scott came up with this recipe for a wine dinner that my dad hosted.
It was paired with a sauvignon blanc and was the runaway hit of the evening.

Avocado Sweet Potato Vichyssoise

1   pound sweet potatoes
1   small carrot, peeled
½   celery stalk
½   small onion
2   ripe avocados, peeled and pitted
¼   cup balsamic vinegar
½   cup olive oil
1   tablespoon brown sugar
1   teaspoon chipotle chilies, minced
2   cups whipping cream
6   drops Tabasco
1   teaspoon Worcestershire
1   clove garlic, crushed
     Salt and pepper to taste
1   corn tortilla, cut into julienne strips
     Vegetable oil for frying
½   pound mixed baby greens
1   dozen large cooked shrimp, chilled
     Serves 6

1 Place the sweet potatoes, carrot, celery, and onion in a pot and cover with water. Boil until tender. Drain and cool.

2 Transfer the ingredients to a food processor, add avocados and balsamic vinegar, and puree. While the processor is on, slowly add the olive oil, sugar, chipotle chilies, cream, Tabasco, Worcestershire, garlic, and salt and pepper to taste. Transfer to a bowl and refrigerate for at least one hour.

3 In the meantime, fry the tortilla strips in vegetable oil for the garnish. When the soup is chilled, ladle the soup into individual bowls and top with the baby greens, the chilled shrimp, and the tortilla strips. Drizzle some oil from the chipotle chili can over the top and serve.

Leeks add a terrific flavor to this wonderful soup...and now you'll have another great use for leftover baked potatoes other than potato salad.

Baked Potato Soup

2   tablespoons butter

1½ cups leeks, cleaned thoroughly
     and finely diced

2   cloves garlic, crushed

6   cups Chicken Stock (pg 24)

4   large baked potatoes, smashed,
     or better yet, put through a ricer

1   cup buttermilk

1   cup sour cream

½   cup grated Parmesan cheese

½   cup grated cheddar cheese

¼   cup minced chives

     Salt and pepper to taste

     Cooked bacon bits for garnish

     Serves 4

1 In a large pot, melt the butter and
   sweat the garlic and the leeks until
   soft. Add the stock and heat to a boil.

2 In a separate bowl, whisk together
   the potatoes, buttermilk, sour cream,
   Parmesan, cheddar, and chives. Add
   the mixture to the soup, stirring constantly with a whisk. Season with salt
   and pepper. Serve garnished with
   bacon bits, chives, and some extra
   shredded cheddar cheese.

Feel free to experiment with whatever you find in your garden or at the farmer's market. For it to be real Spanish gazpacho, however, you cannot omit the bread or the olive oil. Also, you can add hot peppers, but a Spaniard would probably leave them out.

Gazpacho

4   ripe tomatoes, peeled and chopped

2   garlic cloves, crushed

     Dash of salt

1   slice hearty white bread, crust
     removed, torn into crumbs

1   tablespoon red wine vinegar

1   cucumber, peeled, seeded and chopped

1   green pepper, cleaned and chopped

2   tablespoons extra-virgin olive oil

4   cups tomato juice

     Salt and fresh ground pepper to taste

2   tablespoons scallions, diced

     Serves 4

1 In a medium nonreactive bowl, add
   garlic and a little salt and work into
   a paste with the bread crumbs and
   vinegar. Add three of the tomatoes
   and mash as fine as possible.

2 Mix the puree with the remaining
   tomato, cucumber, and green pepper
   and chill. Before serving, stir in the
   olive oil and tomato juice. Add more
   vinegar if desired and salt and pepper
   to taste. Serve garnished with scallions.

There is no such thing as a good cut of meat versus a bad cut of meat. Stew meat is actually more flavorful than steak and is fall-apart tender if cooked properly. Venison is no exception.

Venison Ragout

3   pounds venison stew meat, either shank or neck

1   large onion, sliced

2   tablespoons chopped garlic

1   tablespoon dried thyme

2   tablespoons black peppercorns

6   crushed juniper berries

2   bay leaves

1   bottle red wine

1½ cup flour, seasoned with salt and pepper

½   pound thick-cut bacon, diced

¼   cup vegetable oil

1   cup Beef Stock or beef broth (pg 24)

2   tablespoons Dry Barbecue Rub (pg 25)

Serves 8

1   Place the stew meat in a glass bowl with the onion, garlic, thyme, peppercorns, juniper berries, bay leaves, and red wine. Cover the meat and let it marinate in the refrigerator for 24 hours.

2   Remove the stew meat from the bowl and pat dry. Strain the red wine and reserve. Save the onions for cooking.

3   In a large pan, fry the bacon until the fat is rendered. With a slotted spoon, remove the bacon and add to a large pot. Dredge the stew meat in the flour and brown in the bacon fat. Brown the meat in batches so you don't overcrowd the pan, and add a little vegetable oil if needed. When the meat is brown, add to the pot. Brown the onions. Add the red wine to the pan and scrape all the flavorful bits off the bottom of the pan. Pour the red wine over the meat and onions in the pot and add the Beef Stock and Barbecue Rub. Simmer the ragout, covered, for 1½–3 hours until fork tender, depending on the age of the deer. Serve with Spaetzle (pg 140) or Cheddar Mashed Potatoes (pg 136).

A STRAIGHTFORWARD AMERICAN MENU

Like the restaurant itself, the Schuler's menu has undergone significant changes over the years. While some staples such as the Prime Rib remain from the early days, both the pricing and the composition of the restaurant's offerings are different from Albert Schuler's Blue Plate Special or the British-inspired menu of the Win Schuler days. ◆ In 1959, for example, a complete Schuler's dinner ranged from $1.75 for scallops to $3.25 for sirloin steak. And an Old English script luncheon menu ("for groups of 20 or more") from the '60s offered entrees ranging from London Broil to Shank of Lamb and Chicken Cordon Bleu. ◆ Changing times, dining habits, and dietary considerations have resulted in menu changes as Schuler's has kept pace with the times. ◆ In the spring of 1970 the Schuler's newsletter, the *Inn-Sign-ia*, announced "a dramatic new dinner menu," which included a larger selection of unusual items, and a lowering of entrée prices. "Current social, economic, and dietary conditions suggest a new approach for the food service business," noted the article. The new menu, it was reported, was responding to a more realistic approach to customer satisfaction. ◆ Today, in addition to the Schuler's "Signature Dishes," the menu has taken a lighter turn and now includes "heart-healthy" offerings and options to meet today's lifestyle. Three decades after the restaurant reported dramatic menu changes, the notation "Healthy and Fresh, with sauces available on the side," demonstrates Schuler's continuing commitment to respond to today's "changing social, economic, and dietary conditions."

I call this State Fair Lamb Stew because when I lived in Indianapolis there was a local grocer who would buy fair lamb for his shelves. It was reassuring to get locally raised, "free-range" lamb. This recipe makes good use of it. If you have never cooked with these spices before, you will see how naturally they pair with lamb.

State Fair Lamb Stew

1   pound lamb shoulder, diced
1   pound chicken thighs, diced
2   cloves garlic
1   large onion
1   cup chickpeas
1½ quart chicken stock
½   teaspoon turmeric
½   teaspoon ginger
½   teaspoon ground coriander
1   teaspoon cinnamon
2   (14-ounce) cans crushed tomatoes
1   cup dry lentils, rinsed
    Fresh cilantro for garnish
    Serves 4

1   Preheat the oven to 350°.

2   In a large skillet, brown the lamb and the chicken thighs in olive oil. Transfer to a large pot. Soften the onion and garlic in some more olive oil and transfer them to the pot as well. Add the chickpeas, chicken stock, turmeric, ginger, coriander, cinnamon, tomatoes, and lentils. Stir together and cover. Place everything in the oven and bake until the lentils are done and the lamb is tender, about 1–1½ hours. Add a little water if the stew becomes too thick. Serve in bowls with chopped fresh cilantro for garnish.

Schuler's Executive Chef reviews the menu while line cooks and wait staff look on in late 1940s.

Pumpkin Bisque

I	small carrot, peeled
½	onion, peeled, large chop
I	stalk celery, large chop
6	cups chicken broth
I	24-ounce can packed pumpkin
½	teaspoon nutmeg
I	teaspoon cinnamon
¼	cup honey
¼	pound butter (I stick)
2	cups heavy cream
¼	cup brown sugar
2	ounces dark molasses
½	cup applesauce
	Salt and pepper to taste
½	cup pumpkin seeds, peeled or unpeeled, toasted

Serves 6

1 Boil the carrot, onion, and celery in the chicken broth until the vegetables are tender. Remove the vegetables from the stock and puree in a food processor. Return the vegetables to the chicken stock. Add the pumpkin, nutmeg, cinnamon, honey, butter, cream, brown sugar, molasses, and applesauce and simmer for about 30 minutes. If the soup becomes too thick, simply add water or a little more cream. Salt and pepper to taste.

2 Serve hot with a dollop of sour cream and some toasted pumpkin seeds sprinkled over the soup.

So much mediocre mushroom soup has been prepared over the years that we may have lost sight of how terrific a good bowl can be. This recipe will make believers out of the most jaded soup snob at your next dinner party!

Mushroom Bisque

I	pound fresh mushrooms
I	quart chicken broth
I	medium onion, chopped
7	tablespoons butter
6	tablespoons flour
3	cups milk
I	cup heavy cream
	Kosher salt and white pepper to taste
	Tabasco sauce
2	tablespoons sherry

1 Wash the mushrooms and cut off the stems. Finely chop the stems and toss them, with the chopped onion, in the chicken broth. Cover and simmer for about 30 minutes.

2 Slice the caps and sauté them over medium-high heat in 1 tablespoon of the butter. Reserve them for garnish.

3 Melt the remaining butter in a saucepan over medium-low heat and add the flour, stirring with a whisk to make a roux. Whisk repeatedly until the roux starts to smell like popcorn. (At this point, you know that your soup will not taste like flour.) This will take about five minutes. Add the milk and turn up the heat. Stir constantly until the sauce becomes thickened and smooth. Add the cream.

4 Combine the mushroom broth mixture with the sauce and season to taste with the salt, white pepper and Tabasco. Add the sherry just prior to serving and garnish with the sliced mushrooms.

Pumpkin Bisque

Michigan Bean and Vegetable Soup

½ cup dried lima beans

½ cup dried red kidney beans

½ cup green split peas

½ cup dried navy beans

½ cup dried black-eyed peas

½ cup pinto beans

1 tablespoon butter

1 small onion, diced

2 stalk celery, diced

1 large carrot, diced

1 red pepper, diced

1 gallon chicken stock

2 smoked ham hocks

1 teaspoon dried thyme

2 cloves minced garlic

1 tablespoon whole pepper corn

2 bay leaves

4 parsley stems

Cheesecloth and kitchen twine for sachet bag

Makes one gallon

1 Rinse all of the beans in cold water and combine in a large stockpot. Cover the beans with more cold water and soak them overnight in the refrigerator. In the morning, drain the beans in a colander.

2 In the same large pot, melt the butter and sauté the onions, celery, carrot and pepper. Add the chicken stock and ham hocks to the pot. Tie up the thyme, garlic, peppercorns, bay leaves, and parsley stems in the cheesecloth and add the sachet bag to the pot. Simmer for one hour. Add the beans to the pot and simmer for approximately one additional hour. The beans need to be tender but not mushy.

3 Remove the hocks and pick the meat off of the bones. Chop the ham and return it to the soup. Salt and pepper to taste. Serve the soup with a sprig of parsley for garnish. This dish is absolutely perfect with the Jalapeño Corn Bread.

Fish and Seafood

Winston J. Schuler 1937

Jean Gould Schuler, mother of Hans, 1939

Hans, Bert and Win discuss new menu designs, 1959.

Win Schuler at home with son, Hans, 1939.

Four Schuler generations: Bert, Win, Hans, and Larry, 1968.

You might not want to try this indoors unless you have a good hood fan.
Otherwise, you could smoke up the whole house.

Blackened Perch with Spicy Remoulade Sauce

2   cups unsalted butter, melted
3   dozen perch fillets at room temperature
6   tablespoons Creole Seasoning (pg 26)
    Serves 6

1 Heat a cast iron skillet as hot as possible on the kitchen stove or on the backyard gas barbecue.

2 Dip the perch fillets in the melted butter, which should be kept in a warm shallow pan. Then sprinkle the Creole Seasoning on both sides of the fillets until they are generously coated. Reserve the excess butter.

3 Place 5–6 fillets in the hot pan but do not overcrowd! Cook over high heat until the underside of the fillet becomes dark brown but not black. Flip the fish and pour 1 teaspoon of butter on top of each fillet. Cook until the underside looks about the same (perhaps one minute more). Repeat with the remaining fillets and serve with lemon wedges and Spicy Remoulade Sauce (pg 30).

The Perfect Crab Cake with Creole Mustard Sauce

½   cup finely chopped onion
½   cup finely chopped celery
6   tablespoons unsalted butter
1   pound jumbo lump crabmeat, picked over
1½ cup fine fresh bread crumbs
⅓   cup mayonnaise
1   lemon (zest and juice)
½   teaspoon Creole Seasoning (pg 26)
½   teaspoon Worcestershire sauce
    A few drops Tabasco sauce
2   tablespoons minced fresh flat-leafed parsley leaves
    Serves 6

1 In a skillet, cook the onion and celery in 4 tablespoons of butter over moderately low heat, stirring, until tender, and transfer to a bowl. Stir in the crab and 1 cup of the bread crumbs. In a small bowl, whisk together the mayonnaise, lemon juice and zest, Creole Seasoning, Worcestershire sauce, Tabasco sauce, parsley, salt, and pepper to taste and stir into the crab mixture until well combined.

2 Line a baking sheet with waxed paper. Form crab mixture into 6 flattened rounds, each about 3 inches wide and ¾ inches thick. Pat into remaining bread crumbs in a shallow bowl and transfer to the baking sheet. Chill crab cakes, covered with plastic wrap, at least 1 hour and up to 4.

3 In a heavy skillet, heat 2 tablespoons of butter over moderate heat until the foam subsides, and cook half of the crab cakes until golden brown, about 2–3 minutes on each side. Cook the other cakes in the remaining butter in the same manner. Serve the crab cakes warm with lemon wedges and Creole Mustard Sauce (pg 29).

Perfect Crab Cake with Creole Mustard Sauce

Prepared in this manner, tuna is meaty, satisfying but light, and tastes wonderful.
Get the best tuna steak you can find for this recipe.

Pan-Fried Tuna Steak with an Asian Cucumber Sauce

Steaks

6   tuna steaks (about 6 ounces each—
    1 inch thick)
1   tablespoon black peppercorn
1   teaspoon Chinese five-spice powder
½   teaspoon salt
3   tablespoons olive oil

Cucumber Sauce

1   cucumber
¾   teaspoon salt
2   teaspoon sugar
½   teaspoon red pepper flakes
3   tablespoons cider vinegar
⅓   cup canola or safflower oil
2   teaspoons soy sauce
½   cup water
    Serves 6

1 Smash the peppercorns on a work surface with a rolling pin or the bottom of a pan. Stir the Chinese five-spice powder with the peppercorns on the work surface and press the tuna steaks onto the mixture, coating them on both sides. Sprinkle the steaks with salt.

2 Heat a large skillet until very hot. Add the oil to coat the bottom of the pan and add the steaks. Cook 1 minute on each side just to brown. At this point the steaks are rare. Cook slightly longer if desired. Be careful! Tuna steak shouldn't be served past medium rare, or it loses much of its character. Rare is better than medium in this case.

For sauce

3 Peel the cucumber, de-seed it, and place it in the food processor with the rest of the sauce ingredients. Pulse until the sauce is fine but not completely liquefied. Transfer the sauce to a serving dish and let your guests help themselves.

Ability is a poor man's

— Wren

This recipe utilizes the "Standard Breading Procedure," one of the first things a student learns at any culinary school. Flour, egg wash, and then bread crumbs…and you are ready to fry. This suggestion on how to prepare the Great Lakes' most prized pan fish originates from my friend and Master Chef Milos Cilhelka, who demonstrates that some of the most sublime results in the kitchen often come from seemingly mundane techniques. Note: I can only find hazelnuts in my neighborhood health food store. If you can't find them at your local grocery, experiment with pecans or almonds or just about any other kind of nut. This recipe makes a great breading for trout, too!

Hazelnut Crusted Walleye

2   walleye fillets

½   cup flour, seasoned with salt and pepper

2   eggs, beaten with a little milk

¼   cup fresh bread crumbs

¼   ground hazelnuts

Clarified butter or vegetable oil for frying

Lemon

Serves 2

1 Mix the breads crumbs and the hazelnuts together. Prepare the fish by dredging it in the flour, dipping it in the egg wash, and coating the fillets with the bread crumb/hazelnut mixture.

2 Heat a heavy skillet over medium-high heat and fry the walleye fillets in clarified butter until the crust is a golden brown. Flip the fish and repeat on the other side. The flesh of the fish should be white all the way through, but not dry and flaky. Serve with lemon wedges for garnish.

This dish is a simple, delicious, edible luxury. Size the recipe down and cook it for your sweetheart on Valentine's Day to prove that you realize how lucky you are. Extra bonus points for serving this with a full, buttery Chardonnay. Major bonus points if you follow it with the Chocolate Bread Pudding for dessert!

Classic Coquille St. Jacques

1   pound large sea scallops
1   cup dry vermouth
2   tablespoons butter
1   tablespoon olive oil
1   tablespoon crushed fresh garlic
1   cup heavy whipping cream
1/3 cup Gruyère cheese
2   tablespoons chopped scallions
1/2 teaspoon salt
    White pepper to taste
1   package Pepperidge Farm
    puff pastry squares
    Serves 6–8

1   Marinate the scallops in ¼ cup of the dry vermouth. Set scallops aside for 20 minutes until the puff pastry is done. Bake six to eight of the puff pastry squares, depending on the appetite of your sweetheart, and according to the package directions. (These should be the kind of pastry squares that puff into silos that you can fill with the scallop mixture.) Set aside and keep warm.

2   Add the butter and oil together in a large skillet over medium-high temperature. Gently add the scallops, and leave them undisturbed until they loosen and become lightly browned on the underside. Turn the scallops and repeat. Imagine heating them through rather than cooking them. This will keep them from becoming rubbery. Remove from the pan and set aside on a plate.

3   Add garlic and cook for a few seconds. Burned garlic will ruin the dish. Pull the pan away from the stove and add the vermouth. Return the pan to the stove and let it flame! Let the flame burn until nearly extinguished. Add the cream and cook until the volume in pan is reduced by one-half. Stir in the cheese, salt and pepper to taste, and add the scallops to warm for a few seconds.

4   Pour into the warm puff pastry shells and garnish with chopped scallions. Enjoy!

Broiled Whitefish with Herbed Butter

2 whitefish fillets, big enough to
satisfy your appetite
olive oil
Kosher salt and pepper to taste
dash of paprika

4 ounces Herbed Butter (pg 29)
chopped parsley for garnish

Serves 2

1 Preheat your oven broiler. Coat the whitefish fillets with olive oil and season with the salt and pepper. Sprinkle a little dash of paprika on for a little added flavor and color. Broil the fish until the middle is white but not dry. With a broiler, you'll have to keep a close eye on the fish to keep it from burning.

Serve with a scoop of the Herbed Butter melting over each fillet, a bit of chopped parsley and a chilled glass of Chardonnay. Also goes great with Cheddar Mashed Potatoes (pg 136).

This recipe is very simple and takes less time to prepare than you would think. The beets and the potatoes can be roasting while you are prepping the grill and cooking the fish. The entire dish can be ready in 40 minutes.

Grilled Salmon with Balsamic Vinegar Roasted Beets

2   salmon fillets
    Olive oil
    Salt and pepper
4   medium-sized beets
4   Yukon Gold potatoes
2   tablespoons balsamic vinegar
1   teaspoon dried thyme
2   tablespoons crème fraiche
1   small bunch Italian parsley for garnish
    Serves 2

1   Preheat the oven to 400°. Preheat the grill.

2   Peel the beets and cut them in half, leaving the stems on for presentation. Clean the Yukon Gold potatoes and slice them into thick disks or halves. Toss the beets and potatoes in separate bowls with balsamic vinegar, olive oil, salt, pepper, and thyme. Place the beets and potatoes on a sheet tray and roast for approximately 30 minutes.

3   Brush the salmon with olive oil, and salt and pepper. Cook on a hot grill until the outside of the fish is crispy, but the inside is still pink. To serve, place the Italian parsley in a dinner bowl, and then add the salmon, crème fraiche, beets, and potatoes. Drizzle with more vinegar and oil if desired. Try this dish with a pinot noir instead of a white wine. The bold flavor of the salmon and the beets needs a stronger wine to stand up to it.

"En papillote" means "in paper." This dish sounds complicated, but it is really quite easy, and the presentation is very elegant. This dish should definitely be put in the "romantic dinner for two" file.

Halibut en Papillote

2   halibut fillets (about 6 ounces each)
    Pinch cayenne pepper
2   large sheets parchment paper
1   tomato, chopped
½   cucumber, peeled, seeded, and sliced thin
½   cup button mushrooms, sliced
½   onion, sliced
1   ounce white wine
    Salt and pepper to taste
    2 sprigs fresh dill
    Serves 2

1   Preheat the oven to 350°.

2   Dust the halibut with a pinch of cayenne pepper. Put the parchment on a baking sheet and lay the fish in the middle of each paper square. Sauté the tomatoes, cucumber, mushrooms, onion, and wine together in a sauté pan until the vegetables are just starting to get tender. Salt and pepper to taste.

3   Spoon the vegetable mixture over the halibut and top it with the dill. Fold the paper together and hand seam the edges, so the bag is very tight. Bake in the oven until the bags puff. If you have done a good job sealing your bags, the puffing will indicate that the fish is done.

4   You and your guest should not cut into the paper until the dish has reached the table, so you can enjoy the aroma and the visual appeal of the steam rising out of your "papillote." You can substitute almost any kind of fish in this dish.

Not by age but by capacity is

— Plautus

If you are squeamish about cutting up a live lobster, then buy the frozen lobster tails and thaw them in your refrigerator. To make this dish easier, prepare everything ahead of time and line the ingredients up on your counter in the order they go into the pan, the process becomes much easier.

Lobster Paprikas

2   lobster tails or one whole lobster, meat removed and cut into large chunks

2   tablespoons butter

½   cup green onions, thinly sliced

1   cup mushrooms, washed and quartered

½   cup white wine

½   cup brandy

¼   cup finely diced onions

   Zest and juice from one lemon

2   cloves garlic

1   cup heavy whipping cream

1½ teaspoons good Hungarian paprika

2   tablespoons sour cream

2   tablespoons Parmesan cheese

   Salt and pepper to taste

Serves 2

1   In a large skillet over medium-high heat, sauté the lobster tails, green onions, and mushrooms in butter until the lobster is half cooked. Remove the lobster meat with a slotted spoon and reserve. Away from the flame, add the wine, brandy, onions, garlic, and lemon. Reduce by half. Add the heavy cream, reduce again by half, and finish by whisking in the paprika, sour cream, and Parmesan cheese. Return the lobster to the pan and heat through. Serve with Grilled Sourdough Toast Points (pg 52) garnished with chopped scallions.

wisdom acquired.

*Hand made pasta is easier than it looks, but I think that is partially true because
I have a mechanical pasta roller.*

Lobster and Peas with Saffron Pasta

1	cup all-purpose flour
2	eggs
	Olive oil
	Pinch of saffron
2	lobster tails, flesh removed
1	clove garlic, crushed
¾	cup fresh peas
½	cup water
½	stick cold butter, cut into 4 pieces (higher quality butter is best)
1	tablespoon chopped fresh chives
	Shaved Parmesan for garnish

Serves 2

1 In your food processor, pulse the flour, eggs, a touch of olive oil, and a pinch of saffron until an elastic dough ball is formed. Remove the dough, cover it with plastic wrap, and let it rest for 30 minutes before rolling. Start at the thickest setting and pass the dough through the roller. Fold the dough in half, rotate 90 degrees, and pass it through the next smallest setting, etc. Repeat until you reach the smallest setting. Place the sheet onto a floured surface and cut the dough into wide ribbons. Start a pan of boiling salted water and plunge the pasta in the water about the same time you are plunging the peas in the next step. Cook the pasta until just tender.

2 In a medium-sized skillet, heat some olive oil and sauté the lobster tail meat until it is just barely heated through. Overcooking lobster will make it tough. Set the lobster aside and keep it warm. Add garlic to the pan and soften. Add fresh peas and water. Boil peas until tender (this doesn't take long with fresh peas). Remove with a slotted spoon and keep warm with the lobster.

3 There should still be about ¼ cup of water in the pan. Slowly whisk the cold butter into the water to make a butter fondue. Salt and pepper to taste. Remove the sauce and toss with the lobster, peas, and fresh pasta. Garnish with chopped chives and shaved Parmesan. Serve with a rich, buttery Chardonnay.

Farm-raised mussels are so readily available these days and so inexpensive that I use them regularly.
Buy the live ones at the seafood counter, if possible, since they make a better broth than the precooked variety.

Mussels in a White Wine Broth over Spaghetti

1½ pounds live mussels
  (discard mussels with open shells)
  Olive oil
4 cloves garlic, crushed
½ cup dry white wine
1 cup fish stock
2 tablespoons fresh herbs
  (dill and parsley are good)
  Pinch saffron threads
2 small handfuls dried spaghetti
  Parmesan shavings for garnish
  Salt and pepper to taste
  Serves 2

1 Bring a large pot of salted water to a rapid boil. Throw in the pasta and cook "al dente."

2 In a large skillet, heat some olive oil and soften some garlic. Add the mussels and white wine. Boil off the alcohol and add the fish stock, herbs, and saffron threads. Cover the pan and simmer until the mussel shells are open. Discard the ones that refuse to open.

3 Drain the pasta, and portion into shallow dinner bowls. Divide the mussels over the top of the spaghetti, pour over the broth, and garnish with shaved Parmesan and more chopped parsley. Serve with French bread for sopping up the broth and a white Bordeaux.

HORSES, TENPINS, AND DINING ROOMS
In 1940, Win Schuler added the Frontier Room to the property that his father had turned over to him and his brother. This was the first expansion of the restaurant, and it would be the precursor of several significant changes over the coming years. ◆ The space that today houses the legendary Centennial Room in the Marshall restaurant began as a livery stable, then became a garage, and eventually a bowling alley. Built in the 1930s, the bowling alley had been a neighborhood fixture and drew some regular customers, but it also took up a great deal of space. Ironically, a pinboy strike in 1946 led Win Schuler to conclude that the bowling alley was no longer a profitable venture, and he decided to replace the lanes with a dining room to meet expanding customer demand. ◆ Using lumber from the north woods and a regional sawmill, Schuler's worked around postwar building restrictions and lumber shortages, and the Centennial Room took shape. The new dining room featured murals of historic Marshall and hardwood beams. The terracing of the restaurant up to the level of the kitchen became a Schuler's design trademark, as did the checkered tablecloths, which added to the comfortable atmosphere of the main dining room. ◆ When the upholstery shop next door became available, it was acquired by the restaurant, allowing Schuler's to add a bar, a gift shop (called "The Old Curiosity Shop" and run by Win's wife, Jean), and another dining area that was decorated in the style of Victorian England and called the "Dickens Room." In the 1970s the space was redecorated in "chic, contemporary decor" that gave the renamed "Inner Circle" the comfortable, elegant look. Today, the space has again been redone as the Lodge— an extension of Winston's Pub with a rustic outdoors theme.

This dish has been given the seal of approval from my friend Patxi Garcia, who hails from Pamplona, Spain. I think he was a bit surprised that a Michigan boy could successfully prepare his national dish. As Patxi would remind you, paella is not spicy like jambalaya. So, for an authentic experience, avoid the hot peppers and the spicy sausage that our American palates might expect in this dish.

Seafood Paella

Olive oil

6   bacon slices, thick-cut

8   chicken thighs

2   large onions, chopped

4   garlic cloves, crushed

2   cups long-grained white rice

1   small jar roasted pimentos, sliced

½   teaspoon saffron threads

2   cups clam juice

1½ cups chicken broth

1   pound uncooked shrimp, peeled and deveined

1   pound squid, cleaned

1   dozen clams

1   dozen mussels

1   cup green peas

Lemon wedges

Chopped parsley

Serves 6–8

1   Preheat oven to 350°.

2   In a large heavy pot, brown the bacon in the olive oil until crisp. Remove the bacon with a slotted spoon and set it aside. Sprinkle the chicken with salt and pepper and brown it in the bacon fat. Remove the chicken and set it aside. Add the chopped onion and garlic to the pot and soften. Stir in the rice with the pimentos and saffron. Add the clam juice and chicken stock to the pot and bring the mixture to a simmer. Remove from the heat.

3   Pour the rice mixture into a glass casserole dish (a paella dish would even be better!) and arrange the chicken, shrimp, squid, clams, and mussels in the rice mixture. Sprinkle with the chopped bacon and peas and cover with foil.

4   Bake the paella until the chicken is cooked through and the rice is tender. Discard any mussels or clams that have not opened. Let the dish stand for a few minutes and sprinkle with chopped parsley. Serve with lemon wedges for garnish.

This would be an ideal dish to try if you have one of those fish-grilling contraptions (the ones that hold your fillet in a cage for grilling). This tool allows the flame and smoke to lick the trout without the fish falling apart while you try to turn it. This recipe seems even better if you catch your trout with a fly rod and use your fish-grilling contraption over a crackling fire...hey, we all need something to aim for!

Herb-Stuffed Trout with Horseradish Cream Sauce

2   whole fresh trout, gutted and scaled,
    with the backbone removed
    Olive oil
    Salt and pepper
2   handfuls of fresh herbs
    (dill, parsley, tarragon, lavender, sage, etc.)
1   large lemon, sliced thinly
4   ounces Horseradish Cream Sauce (pg 27)
    Serves 2

1 On a cutting board, score the flesh of the fish with a sharp knife. Oil the fish inside and out and sprinkle with the salt and pepper. Fill the cavity of the fish with the herbs and the lemon. Rub a few of the herbs into the scoring, too. Secure the fish in the grilling cage and cook over red-hot coals.

2 Cook until the flesh is past translucent, but not overly flakey. The fish should still be very moist. Serve with the Horseradish Cream Sauce and, for campers, a potato that has been baking in the campfire. Beer optional.

Typical scene of the 1870's, now the Paul Herman Hardware Store. Pedestrians competed with merchandise for right-of-way.

Poultry and Meat

This recipe is so simple, and it makes terrific use of whatever herbs are ready in your home herb boxes or that you can find in your local grocery's produce section. I created this dish for my daughters using my favorite herb, tarragon, with a little marjoram thrown in for good measure. Serve it with some mashed sweet potatoes and roasted asparagus.

Center Cut Pork Chops with a Dijon Cream Sauce   {TITLE PAGE PHOTO}

4   6-ounce boneless pork loin chops
2   tablespoons butter
¼   cup finely diced onion
1   clove fresh garlic, crushed
⅓   cup dry white wine
½   cup chicken or pork stock
1   teaspoon Dijon mustard
½   cup cream
2   teaspoons chopped fresh herbs like tarragon, lavender, marjoram, sage, or rosemary

Serves 4

1   Salt and pepper the pork loins. Heat a sturdy saucepan over medium-high heat, add butter and place the cuts of pork in the pan. The pan should be hot enough to hear the pork sizzle, but not so hot that it smokes. Cook the chops 3–4 minutes on each side or until brown and cooked through. Pork chops should still be tender to the touch and slightly pink in the middle when they are done, not cooked through to the consistency of shoe leather. Remove the pork and set aside.

2   Add the onion to the pan and cook for a minute (scraping up the flavorful bits on the bottom of the pan). Add the garlic and sauté for 30 additional seconds. Do not burn the garlic! Turn the heat to high and add the wine. Let the mixture go almost dry in the pan. Add the stock and let that reduce by half. Add the cream and the mustard. Cook until the sauce is thickened and stir in the fresh herbs. Finally, add the pork chops to warm in the sauce before plating.

Win Schuler accepting one of Schuler's 37 consecutive Travel Holiday Awards.
Michigan State University Athletic Director Biggie Munn does the honors.

Marinated Breast of Chicken Dakota

8   6-ounce chicken breasts

Marinade

2   cups pineapple juice

2   cups apple juice

1   cup brown sugar

1   cup soy sauce

¼   cup Worcestershire sauce

4   garlic cloves, minced

2   lemons, halved and juiced

1   cup salad oil

½   cup parsley stems, chopped

2   bay leaves

1   tablespoon ground ginger

Serves 8

1   Combine all of the marinade ingredients in a large bowl and submerge the chicken breasts. Refrigerate overnight in a covered container before preparing the chicken for the grill.

2   Grill the chicken breasts over medium-high heat until they are firm, but not tough. Let the dish stand a few minutes before serving.

THAT OLD SCHOOL SPIRIT   Sports and eating often seem to go hand-in-hand, and Schuler's has had its share of both. ♦ Winston Schuler was quarterback of the 1929 Albion College football team, which defeated Michigan State University by a score of 2–0 (with Win tackling the opposing quarterback in the end zone for a safety). The small Michigan college later won the MIAA conference championship, and Win Schuler's 65-yard run in the fourth quarter helped win the final game for the "purple and gold." Win's active participation in sports spanned 25 years, as he combined the family business with officiating at football and basketball games and at colleges and high schools across the Midwest, as did son Hans in the early 1960s. ♦ Refereeing basketball games, teaching, and traveling also resulted in loyalty. "We're coming down to see you in your little restaurant," wrote one friend from the Upper Peninsula, soon after Win had moved to Marshall to take over the hotel and restaurant for his father in the 1930s. ♦ On a larger collegiate stage, the Big Ten Conference (primarily Midwestern universities such as Michigan, Michigan State, Purdue, Indiana, and Ohio State) and noteworthy independents such as Notre Dame have many fans who are loyal Schuler's restaurant patrons. For decades during the fall football season, Marshall has been referred to as the "Crossroads of the Big Ten." Partisan support of one's alma mater is often thirsty work, and, of course, there are few places better suited to debating the relative merits of your favorite team than a restaurant and watering hole. It's no wonder, then, that Midwestern collegiate coaches and teams have been attracted to Schuler's over the years. Duffy Daugherty, Biggie Munn, Bump and Pete Elliott, Ara Parshegian, Bo Schembechler, Don Canham, George Perles, and Tom Izzo are just a few of the Big Ten coaches who have frequented the restaurant. ♦ For a number of years, one of the restaurant's rooms was called the Stadium Room. Pictures and remembrances of fans and athletes from a wide range of sports continue to grace the walls of Schuler's.

This may be the ultimate comfort food. Serve with Yukon Gold Smashed Potatoes with Garlic and Chives and tender green peas and you'll be reminded of dishes "like mother used to serve." Or, if your mother didn't cook like mine, go ahead and try this recipe on a cool fall evening, and start a tradition that your family will remember in the years to come.

Beef Short Ribs Braised in Red Wine

5   pounds beef short ribs, cut into
    1-rib pieces if necessary

4   garlic cloves, chopped

6   small onions (about 1 pound total),
    unpeeled but chopped

6   carrots, sliced

2   bay leaves

½   teaspoon dried rosemary, crumbled
    (or 1 teaspoon fresh)

1   cup red wine

    All-purpose flour seasoned with
    salt and pepper for dredging

⅛   cup rendered bacon fat
    (olive oil may also be used)

1   teaspoon Hungarian paprika

2   cups Beef Stock (pg 24) or low-sodium
    canned beef broth

Garnish

½   cup finely chopped parsley
    Zest of 1 lemon

2   large clove garlic, finely chopped

Serves 6

1   Marinate the ribs overnight in the wine, garlic, onions, carrots, bay leaves, and rosemary. Lay short ribs flat in a glass baking pan and pour the marinade ingredients over the top. Cover with plastic wrap and refrigerate overnight.

2   Preheat oven to 350°. Remove the ribs from marinade and pat dry. Reserve the liquid. Dredge ribs in flour, knocking off excess. Heat the bacon fat or olive oil in a 6-quart heavy ovenproof kettle over moderately high heat until hot, but not smoking. Brown the short ribs in batches (in a single layer without crowding). Transfer the ribs as browned with tongs to a large plate.

3   Pour off all but about 2 tablespoons of the fat remaining in the kettle and in it cook the strained garlic, onions, carrots, bay leaves, and rosemary from the marinade plus the paprika over moderate heat, stirring, until lightly browned. Add the reserved wine to the pan to deglaze. (As always, make sure to loosen all of the flavorful brown bits off the bottom of the pan.) Cook for a minute or two to evaporate the alcohol and then add the broth. Bring to a boil.

4   Return ribs to kettle, in a single layer, if possible, and cover the kettle with a lid. Braise the ribs in the oven until tender, about 2 hours.

5   Transfer the ribs with tongs to a platter and keep them warm. Pour the cooking liquid through a fine sieve set over a saucepan, discarding the solids, and skim the fat. If necessary, boil the liquid to thicken it slightly, and spoon the sauce over the ribs.

Garnish

6   Combine the ingredients at the last minute to ensure freshness and sprinkle them over the top of the ribs when plating. The zesty, fresh flavor of this garnish will offset the deep richness of the beef to bring the dish into perfect balance.

Michigan's Upper Peninsula is known for its meat "pasties"—a creation similar to a pot pie, but much more delicious and complex. My grandmother had her own version, which I recreate here. I like to serve any kind of savory pie with a nice green salad drizzled in a tart vinaigrette dressing. The acidity of the dressing helps to cut the fat from the pie dough, creating a perfectly balanced harmony of flavors on the palate. This dish would be terrific served with a dry Riesling or a Cote du Rhone (if you prefer a glass of red).

Grandma Schuler's Cornish Pasties

1   pound Grandma's Pie Crust (pg 155)

½   pound finely diced sirloin

½   pound finely diced pork steak

1   large russet potato, peeled
    and finely diced

1   small rutabaga, finely diced

1   medium onion, finely diced

1   tablespoon parsley, finely chopped

½   teaspoon kosher salt

½   teaspoon freshly ground black pepper

1   tablespoon flour

1   tablespoon butter
    (Carrots may be substituted for
    rutabaga if needed.)

Serves 4

1 Preheat oven to 400°.

2 Prepare Grandma's Pie Crust.
   Cover and let rest.

3 Make up the pasty filling by mixing the
   sirloin, pork steak, potato, rutabaga,
   onion, parsley, salt, pepper, and flour.
   Divide the pie dough into four equal
   parts and roll each out onto a floured
   surface. Mound the filling in the center
   of the dough and dot each part with
   butter. Fold the dough over the filling
   and into a half-moon shape, roll the
   edges, and pinch to seal in the filling.
   Cut a slit of your own design in the
   top of the dough to vent and bake for
   30–40 minutes, or until golden brown.

*Hans and Larry Schuler sample an
excellent white wine.*

Cassoulet of Sausages

8   bacon slices, coarsely chopped

3   pounds fully cooked smoked sausages
      (such as kielbasa), cut crosswise
      into ¾-inch-thick rounds

2   medium onions, chopped

6   garlic cloves, chopped

1   tablespoon chopped fresh rosemary

1   tablespoon chopped fresh thyme

½   teaspoon dried crushed red pepper

½   cup brandy

3   15-ounce cans Great Northern
      beans, drained

2   14½ ounce cans diced tomatoes in juice

1   10-ounce package frozen
      baby lima beans, thawed

1   cup Chicken Stock (pg 24) or low-salt
      chicken broth

3   tablespoons tomato paste

½   teaspoon ground allspice

¼   cup olive oil

4   cups coarse fresh bread crumbs
      made from crustless French bread

½   cup freshly grated Parmesan cheese

¼   cup chopped fresh parsley

      Serves 10

1   Preheat oven to 350°.

2   Cook the bacon in a heavy, large ovenproof pot over medium-high heat until brown and crisp, about 4 minutes. Using a slotted spoon, transfer the bacon to a bowl. Add the sausages to the drippings in the pot; sauté until brown, about 15 minutes.

3   Transfer the sausages to a bowl with the bacon. Pour off all but ¼ cup of drippings from the pot. Add the onions and garlic and sauté until the mixture begins to soften, about 10 minutes. Stir in the rosemary, thyme, and crushed red pepper. Add the brandy and simmer until it is nearly evaporated, about 3 minutes. Stir in the canned beans, tomatoes (with juices), lima beans, 1 cup broth, tomato paste, and allspice. Return the sausages and bacon to the pot. Season the cassoulet with salt and pepper. Bring to a boil.

4   Cover the pot and transfer to pre-heated oven; bake for 30 minutes.

5   Increase the oven temperature to 400°. Heat the oil in a large nonstick skillet over medium heat. Add bread crumbs and sauté until light golden brown, about 4 minutes. Transfer to small bowl. Mix in Parmesan cheese; season with salt and pepper. Sprinkle over the warm cassoulet. Bake until the bread crumb topping is a deep golden brown, about 15–20 minutes. Sprinkle the cassoulet with parsley and serve.

We must learn to live together or perish together as fools.

— Dr. Martin Luther King Jr.

The overnight marinade is the key to this dish, along with the quality of the chicken itself. Pay a little more for Amish chicken if it's available in your area, or the Bell and Evans brand if not. The better bird is worth the cost. Given enough time to properly marinate, this dish is almost foolproof. Serve this wonderful bird and flavor-packed potatoes with a tossed green salad laced with a red-wine vinaigrette.

Mediterranean Roast Chicken with Pan Braised Potatoes

½ cup olive oil

2 lemons, juiced and grated zest

4 garlic cloves, peeled and smashed

1 cup apple cider

4 fresh dill sprigs

8 fresh rosemary sprigs

   Kosher salt and freshly ground pepper to taste

2 small chickens (2–2½ pounds each), rinsed well and patted dry

1½ pounds small new red potatoes or small Yukon Gold potatoes, scrubbed and halved

1 cup imported green or black olives

Serves 4

1 Combine the olive oil, lemon juice and zest, garlic, apple cider, rosemary, dill, salt, and pepper in a large bowl. Coat the chickens well and refrigerate them overnight in a covered container.

2 Preheat the oven to 400°.

3 Place the chickens in a large roasting pan.

4 Put the rosemary sprigs, dill, and the garlic from the marinade into the cavity of the chickens. Surround the chickens with the potatoes and olives and drizzle the marinade over everything.

4 Roast the chickens, basting occasionally, until the juices run clear when the thickest part of the thigh is pricked with a knife, about 1 hour. Let the chickens rest for a few minutes before carving.

as brothers

Throughout Schuler's history, this classic has always been among the restaurant's most popular dishes. Until I was about 18, this is the only thing I would order when I ate in the dining room. I often promised myself that I would try something different, but the lure of medium rare prime rib with horseradish cream sauce (and, for me, crispy steak fries) always proved to be too much of a temptation to resist. Even after my palate has become much more sophisticated, I don't think anything can beat a good cut of prime rib. In the years since my youth, the only things that have changed are that the fries have been replaced by steamed redskin potatoes and the Coca-Cola with a glass of hearty Cabernet!

Schuler's Famous Prime Rib

1   oven-ready rib roast (the best you can find—ask the butcher for help!)

3   tablespoons Schuler's Seasoning Salt (pg 30)

1   pound chopped onions, celery and carrots

2   quarts beef broth

Serves 16

1   Season the roast with Schuler's Seasoning Salt. Place vegetables (large chop) in bottom of the roasting pan and put the roast on top of the vegetables.

2   Roast at 350° for approximately 30–45 minutes, or until the surface of the meat is brown. Then turn down the heat to 275° and cook for about two more hours (everyone's oven is different) or until the internal temperature of the meat reaches 125° (when your meat thermometer is inserted at the middle of the rib). At that point, immediately take the prime rib from the oven.

3   Remove the roast from the pan and let it rest for at least 30 minutes in a warm place (covered with aluminum foil) until carving. *Important*—the juices need a chance to return to the middle of the roast and the temperature will continue to rise until the meat is perfectly done!

4   Remove the excess fat from the roasting pan (reserve for making Yorkshire pudding).

5   Heat the pan on the stovetop until the vegetables are browned and the liquid in the pan has evaporated. Add the beef broth and scrape the bottom of the pan, making sure to get the entire flavor into the broth. Simmer a bit so that the veggies can release their flavor into the broth as well. Salt and pepper as necessary.

6   Strain the broth (au jus) into a gravy boat for service.

7   Slice 8 pieces per half roast or 16 pieces for one whole roast.

I love to serve this dish for people who say they don't like venison. Good quality meat is important. Either order it from your local meat market, or, if you are a hunter and harvest your own meat... age it before butchering! Properly hung venison should age 2–4 weeks, depending on the size of the deer, before being skinned and processed. The meat will be more tender and less "gamey."

Venison Loin with a Cognac Cherry Sauce

4   4-ounce medallions of venison
    (from the loin is best)

¼   cup dried Michigan cherries or
    dried sweetened cranberries

1   tablespoon clarified butter or peanut oil

⅓   cup cognac

¼   cup red onion, finely diced

2   garlic cloves, minced

½   cup Beef Stock (pg 24) or beef broth

2   tablespoons cold butter

2   tablespoons fresh tarragon

2   tablespoons chopped scallions for garnish

Serves 4

1 Soak the cherries in the cognac. Set aside for at least 30 minutes. Salt and pepper the medallions of venison and keep them ready by the stove.

2 Heat the oil or butter in a medium-sized saucepan over medium heat until the oil slides easily across the pan. Place the medallions of venison in the pan and sear each side for approximately 2 minutes, or until meat is browned but the inside is still rare. Remove the medallions from the pan and keep them on a plate by the stove.

3 Add the onions to the pan and cook them until they begin to soften. Add garlic and cook for 10–15 seconds, stirring constantly until soft, but not brown. Add the cognac–cherry mixture to the pan and cook until the liquid is reduced by half, or, if the cognac flames, the flame burns itself out. Add the Beef Stock and reduce by half. Finally, add the fresh tarragon and then the cold butter and whisk until the butter is incorporated and the sauce is thickened.

4 Reheat the medallions briefly in the sauce. Serve the venison and the sauce with roasted potatoes and seasonal vegetables. Sprinkle the plate with chopped scallions for garnish.

A very accomplished wine representative in West Michigan once told me that the chemical combination of green peppercorns and red wine provides the same endorphin rush as does chocolate. Purely in the interest of science, I immediately began experimenting with some recipes. If you, too, are intrigued by the science of the peppercorn-wine combination, you may want to serve this simple, lush dish with a full-bodied Cabernet.

Filet of Beef with a Cognac Peppercorn Sauce

2   six- to eight-ounce filet mignons
    Salt and pepper
1   teaspoon clarified butter
    (you may substitute peanut oil)
1   tablespoon finely diced shallots
2   tablespoons green peppercorns, drained
2   tablespoons cognac
¼   cup beef broth
1   tablespoon cold unsalted butter
    Pinch of chopped fresh herbs like chervil, tarragon, or lavender (optional)
Serves 2

1 Preheat the oven to 350°. Uncork the cabernet and let it breathe.

2 In a small skillet on a medium to medium-high stove, heat the clarified butter until it slides easily across the bottom of the pan. Salt and pepper the filets and place them in the pan, being careful not to crowd the beef. There should be a steady sizzle in the pan (not enough to set off the smoke alarm). Brown the filets fully, first on one side, and then the other. At this point, the bigger filets will still be very rare. If that's not the way you like your steak, set the pan in the oven and let the filets cook for another 5 minutes or so until they reach the desired temperature. Remove the filets from the pan and set aside.

3 Sauté the shallots and the peppercorns in the remaining butter in the skillet until the shallots soften (add a touch more butter if you need to). Then take the pan from the stove, add the cognac and return to the heat. Your cognac may or may not flame at this point depending on the heat of your pan and whether or not you cook with gas. Regardless, cook the cognac for a few seconds until the alcohol is burned off and then add the beef broth. Reduce this mixture by half and then whisk in the cold butter to thicken the sauce. Stir in the herbs, if desired, and salt and pepper to taste. Pour the sauce over the filets and serve immediately.

The success of this dish depends on the quality of the chicken you buy and the ripeness of the tomato you use.
If you don't have ripe red tomatoes from the garden, use canned. The inspiration for this dish came from a meal
I had in a small restaurant outside of Lyon, France. A college friend and I were hitchhiking through on our way
south from Strasbourg. We stopped for the night and had a fantastic dinner near the local pension where we stayed.
Typically, I can't remember the name of the town or the restaurant, but I can remember what was in that dish!
For 15 years I have reminisced over the stove while making this treat. Here is as close as I can get to the original.

French Bistro Chicken with Tarragon Tomato Sauce

| whole chicken, cut into 8 pieces
¾   cup flour
| teaspoon salt
| teaspoon black pepper
2   tablespoons olive oil
| medium-sized red onion, finely diced
| teaspoon minced garlic
¼   cup red wine vinegar
½   cup chicken broth
1½ cups tomato concasse
    (or diced canned tomatoes)
| tablespoon chopped fresh tarragon
    (not dried!)
    Serves 5

1 Combine the flour, salt, and pepper in a shallow pan and dredge each piece of the chicken in the flour, making sure to shake off the excess.

2 In a large heavy skillet or Dutch oven, heat the olive oil over medium to medium-high heat until the oil slides easily across the bottom of the pan. Add the chicken to the pan in a single noncrowded layer. (Do this in two batches if you do not have enough space.) Cook the chicken to deep golden brown on each side and set it aside on a platter.

3 Add the onion and the garlic to the pan and cook until slightly softened. This should take only a few seconds. Add the vinegar, turn up the heat, and scrape the flavorful brown bits from the bottom of the pan. Boil the vinegar until it is nearly evaporated. Add the chicken broth and boil until reduced by half. Add the tomato concasse and reintroduce the chicken to the pan. Cover and let the dish simmer on the stove until the chicken is done, perhaps 20 minutes.

4 Remove the chicken to a serving platter, stir the fresh tarragon into the simmering sauce, and pour the sauce over the chicken. Serve with the Yukon Gold Smashed Potatoes (pg 133) and some fresh green beans, et voila!

My first memory of roasted lamb is from a party that my parents threw when I was about five. My dad dug a pit in the backyard, built a huge fire, and spit-roasted a pig and a lamb over the hot coals. Someone was basting the meat all day long. The pork was spectacular, but the lamb stopped me in my tracks. I can still taste it.

Oven-Roasted Marinated Leg of Lamb

1   whole leg of lamb, bone in
    (tell the butcher what you plan and
    he should be able to trim you
    a nice roast)
    Zest and juice from 3 lemons

2   cups olive oil

2   sprigs each—rosemary, dill, sage,
    Greek oregano, and fresh thyme
    Small bunch parsley, chopped
    stems and all

1   bottle dry white wine

¼   cup fresh garlic, crushed
    Salt and fresh ground pepper to taste
    (yes, taste your marinades)

1   stick butter

2½ pounds Yukon Gold potatoes, whole

    Serves 8

1   Whisk the lemon juice, olive oil, herbs, wine, garlic, salt, and pepper together in a stainless steel bowl. (Chop, crush, rip, or bruise the herbs first to release their flavors.)

2   Preheat the oven to 275°.

3   Put the leg of lamb in a double-lined garbage bag and pour the marinade over the meat. Remove as much of the air as possible from the bag and twist it tight, so the marinade surrounds the meat on all sides. Be careful not to rip the bag with the leg bone. Tie off the bag, place it in a pan, and put in the refrigerator for at least 24 hours. By using a bag, you won't have to turn the lamb while marinating.

4   Remove the lamb from the marinade and pat dry. In a heavy-gauge roasting pan, brown the leg in some olive oil over medium-high heat. When all sides are browned, put a grate in the bottom of the pan to lift the roast off of the bottom and pour the marinade over the top of the meat. Add the stick of butter to the pan and place the roast in the oven. Roast slowly, basting every 30–45 minutes until the internal temperature reads 135°, about two hours.

5   Remove the leg from the oven and let it rest at least 20 minutes before carving. Cover the potatoes to keep them hot. Carve some of the meat in the kitchen, place it on a serving platter with the potatoes, and drizzle everything with juices from the pan. For a more traditional presentation, you can bring the show to the table and carve the lamb in front of your guests. This dish pairs perfectly with the Crustless Spinach and Cheese Pie (pg 130). And go ahead and serve that hearty red wine you've been saving for a special occasion. This is definitely the time.

This is not so much a recipe as it is an event. Good ribs require planning and purpose…and a lot of time.
You might as well invite some friends over, fill a cooler full of beer and make it a party.

Jonathan's Barbecued Baby Back Ribs

4   full slabs baby back ribs

3   cups apple cider

1½ cups apple cider vinegar

1   onion, grated

3   tablespoons Worcestershire sauce

2   tablespoons vegetable oil

2   teaspoons ground cinnamon

2   teaspoons ground thyme

2   cups Dry Barbecue Rub (pg 25)

4   cups Schuler's Barbecue Sauce (pg 26)
    Hickory and applewood chunks
    for smoking
    Smoker (I use an electric one)

Serves 4

1 Combine the apple cider, apple cider vinegar, onion, Worcestershire sauce, vegetable oil, cinnamon, and thyme to make a marinade for the ribs. Place the ribs in a garbage bag and pour the marinade over the top. Squeeze out the air and twist-tie the bag until the marinade surrounds the ribs on all sides. Put the ribs on a tray and in the refrigerator, and let them marinate for at least 24 hours.

2 Remove the ribs from the marinade, pat dry, and massage the meat with the dry rub, making sure to cover every inch with the seasoning. Reserve the marinade for mopping (basting). Let the ribs stand at room temperature at least one hour before smoking. While you are waiting, soak the wood chips and heat up the smoker.

3 When the smoker reaches 220°, add the wood chips and the ribs. The temperature will dip in the smoker, so be quick. Ribs should smoke somewhere between 200 and 220°. Mop the ribs with the marinade every 45 minutes to 1 hour, adding a few wood chips when you remove the lid (otherwise, hands off!). The ribs will be ready in about 3–4 hours, or when the meat has pulled about ½ inch from the end of the bone and is tender to the touch.

4 Finally, remove the ribs from the smoker and finish on the grill or in the oven with the barbecue sauce (some even prefer to serve the sauce on the side). Serve with Jalapeño Corn Bread (pg 58) and Schuler's Famous Cole Slaw (pg 37)…and a lot of napkins.

This is the stripped-down, bachelor-easy, version of this dish; and it is just as tasty as anything I've tried. Do it in the oven for a traditional Sunday dinner or let it simmer in a crockpot all day while you are at work. Potatoes and vegetables can be prepared when you get home.

New England Pot Roast

2	pounds beef chuck
2	cups Beef Stock (pg 24) or broth
1	cup Burgundy wine
½	cup Worcestershire sauce
1	tablespoon Kitchen Bouquet
½	teaspoon black pepper
2	cloves garlic, crushed
1	bay leaf

Serves 4

1 Preheat the oven to 350°.

2 Put the beef chuck in a Dutch oven and pour the rest of the ingredients over the top. Cover and cook for three hours or until the meat is fork tender. Serve with Cheddar Mashed Potatoes (pg 136) and Pan Roasted Winter Vegetables (pg 139).

London Broil

1	flank steak
2	cups small button mushrooms, whole
4½	cups apple juice
1½	cups soy sauce
1	ounce fresh ginger, grated
1½	teaspoons butter
1	pint whole button mushrooms
	Salt and pepper to taste
1	cup Beef Stock

Serves 4

1 Place the flank steak and the mushrooms in a large freezer bag and pour in the apple juice, soy sauce, and ginger. Seal, shake, and refrigerate for 24–36 hours.

2 Remove the flank steak and cook on a hot grill until medium-rare. Let the steak rest on a cutting board. Then sauté the mushrooms in the butter in a hot skillet. When the mushrooms have browned, pour in the beef stock and a touch of the marinade and bring to a boil. Salt and pepper as needed. Cut the flank across the grain and serve with the mushrooms and broth over the top.

Medallions of Veal with Scallions and White Wine Sauce

1 pound veal (eye of round or loin)
½ cup flour, seasoned with salt and pepper
2 eggs, beaten with a little water
½ cup fresh bread crumbs
2 tablespoons olive oil
½ cup white wine
2 ounces butter
½ cup fresh chopped scallions
   Salt and pepper to taste
1 teaspoon parsley, chopped fine
   Serves 4

1 Cut the eye of round into ½-inch-thick medallions and tenderize them with a meat pounder between two sheets of plastic wrap to a thickness of ⅛ inch. Dredge the medallions in the flour, egg wash, and bread-crumbs, and set them aside. Heat a large skillet over medium-high heat and fry the medallions in the olive oil until they are golden brown.

2 Remove the veal from the pan and keep it warm. Add the wine to the pan and let it cook until reduced by half. Add butter and continue to cook until the liquid begins to brown. Add chopped scallions and salt and pepper to taste. Serve the medallions over Spaetzle (pg 140) and cover with the pan sauce. Top with braised red cabbage and a sprinkle of parsley for color.

THE LITTLE FUN THINGS WE DO... Throughout the years, Schuler's has made it a habit to use creative promotions to attract guests, build customer loyalty, and recognize longtime guests. ◆ The Pub, for example, has had its share of fun events, ranging from the weekly "Mug Night," which featured a take-home beer stein, to Tax Bash on April 15, and Celebrity Bartenders being chosen. Musical features in the restaurant or pub have been popular and have added to the Schuler's dining experience. Even different means of transportation have been used to bring in guests. Tour buses still come by the hundreds each year, and nearby Brooks Field is another point of entry for some Schuler's customers. Whenever guests fly into Marshall's tiny airport on the outskirts of town, the restaurant accommodates the pilots and their friends by picking them up and bringing them to Schuler's for a sumptuous repast before flying home. ◆ Nor is loyalty limited to guests. A 1989 *Detroit Free Press* article recounted how "hundreds of current and former Schuler's employees" gathered for a reunion in Marshall. ◆ Another group, calling themselves "Schuler's Sweethearts," spent their honeymoons at Schuler's back when the restaurant also offered hotel rooms. In years past, they had a standing invitation to return to toast each other once again at Schuler's.

For you hunters, this is a great way to enjoy those mallard breasts you have in your freezer and don't quite know what to do with. If your wild birds don't provide enough fat to coat your vegetables, go ahead and cheat with a little vegetable oil or rendered bacon fat. For those of you who are buying your duck, they should give off ample fat to brown your vegetables.

Pan Roasted Duck Breast with Winter Vegetables

4   six- to eight-ounce boneless
    duck breasts

2   of each kind of winter vegetables
    you can get your hands on at the store.
    Look for parsnips, turnips, fennel bulbs,
    carrots, and rutabagas. Then clean and
    cut into similar size shapes.

12 pearl onions

½   teaspoon fresh thyme

2   tart apples

1   ounce apple brandy

¼   cup Beef Stock (pg 24)

2   teaspoons cold unsalted butter
    Kosher salt and freshly ground
    black pepper to taste

1   Heat the oven to 375°.

2   Place the duck breasts skin side up on a cutting board. Make shallow crosshatch incisions into the fat without cutting the meat. Heat a large cast iron skillet over medium heat and add the duck breast skin side down. Cook until the skin is crispy and the fat is mostly rendered. Turn and cook for 1 minute more. Remove breasts and set aside. They should be done no more than medium-rare.

3   Add winter vegetables to the pan along with the pearl onions and season with kosher salt and pepper. Cook the vegetables, turning frequently, until they begin to brown. Transfer them to a baking sheet large enough to hold them in a single layer and roast them in the oven. Let them go about 30 minutes and then add your apples, quartered, and let them cook about 15 minutes more.

4   At about the same time you add your apples, put your skillet back on the heat and de-glaze your pan with the apple brandy. (Try cider if you are avoiding the alcohol.) Make sure to scrape up all the brown bits on the bottom of the pan. When the liquid is almost gone, add the stock and let that reduce by half. Finally, add the fresh chopped thyme and whisk in the cold butter. Turn to low and add your breast back into the pan, cover, and reheat. Plate the winter vegetables first, with the duck breast and sauce over the top.

This dish should be illegal served over fried Potato Pancakes (pg 140). Wow!

More...

Wild Mushroom Risotto

6   cups Chicken Stock (pg 24) or
    low-sodium canned chicken broth

3   tablespoons butter

3   tablespoons olive oil

2   shallots, chopped

1   pound assorted wild mushrooms
    (such as oyster, crimini, and
    stemmed shiitake), sliced

1   cup Arborio rice or medium-grain rice

½   cup dry sherry

½   cup freshly grated Parmesan cheese
    (about 2 ounces)

¾   teaspoon chopped fresh thyme

Serves 6

1 Bring the stock to simmer in a medium saucepan. Reduce the heat to low, cover and keep the stock hot.

2 Melt 3 tablespoons of butter with the olive oil in a heavy large saucepan over medium heat. Add the chopped shallots, sauté 1 minute. Add the wild mushrooms and cook until the mushrooms are tender and the juices are released, about 8 minutes. Add the rice and stir to coat. Add sherry and simmer until the liquid is absorbed, stirring frequently, about 8 minutes.

3 Increase the heat to medium-high. Add ¾ cup hot stock and simmer until absorbed, stirring frequently. Add the remaining stock ¾ cup at a time, allowing the broth to be absorbed before adding more, and stirring frequently until the rice is tender and the mixture is creamy, about 20 minutes. Stir in the Parmesan cheese and chopped fresh thyme. Serve warm.

This classic quiche is still my favorite.
A tossed green salad with Herb Vinaigrette will complement it perfectly.

Quiche Lorraine

8   ounces Grandma's Pie Crust (pg 155)

½   pound thick-cut bacon, diced

1   small onion, diced

¼   cup Swiss cheese, grated

4   eggs

1   tablespoon flour

1¼   cups heavy whipping cream

     Pinch nutmeg

½   teaspoon salt

     Fresh ground black pepper to taste

1   tablespoon grated Parmesan cheese

1   teaspoon parsley, finely chopped

Serves 4–6

1 Preheat the oven to 375°.

2 Roll out the dough on a floured surface large enough to fit into a 9-inch pie tin with a little dough hanging over the side. Roll up the excess dough and pinch it together to form a border around the edge of the tin.

3 For the filling, fry the bacon until crisp and drain. Place the bacon in the pastry shell with the Swiss cheese. In a small bowl, whisk together the eggs, flour, cream, nutmeg, salt and pepper. Pour over the bacon and cheese. Sprinkle the top of the quiche with the Parmesan cheese and parsley. Bake for approximately 30 minutes or until the custard is firm and golden, not dry.

As a college student I spent a semester abroad in the food fanatic city of Strasbourg…home of 3 of the 21 Michelin three-star restaurants in France. When my parents visited, I was able to experience these palaces of haute cuisine, but my day-to-day budget was that of a typical student scavenger. This recipe, which can be found at almost any bar in the city, filled me up and left me plenty of francs to pursue my true passion at the time, Alsatian beer and wine. Vive la France!

Tortellini a la Crème with Ham and Mushrooms {PHOTO PG 8}

2   pounds fresh or frozen cheese tortellini
2   tablespoons butter
1   teaspoon minced garlic
1   cup sliced button mushrooms
½   cup asparagus tips
¾   cup heavy whipping cream
½   cup ham, thinly sliced into julienne strips
½   cup freshly grated Parmesan cheese
     Salt and pepper to taste

1 Cook the tortellini in salted, rapidly boiling water until they begin to float to the surface. They should still be springy to the touch. Remove the tortellini from the water and shock them with cold water to stop the cooking process.

2 In a large sauté pan, melt the butter over medium heat. (If you don't have a large pan, you will need to do this in two separate batches.) Add the garlic, mushrooms, asparagus, and ham to the pan and cook until the mushrooms have released their liquid and are beginning to brown. More browning means more flavor, but the trade-off is that the garlic could burn and turn your dish bitter, so be careful!

3 Add the whipping cream, turn up the heat, and let the whipping cream reduce by half. Add the Parmesan and tortellini to the pan and shake, flip, or stir the ingredients around to coat the pasta. Heat the tortellinis through, salt and pepper to taste, and serve immediately. Garnish with a fresh chopped herb of your choosing. Experience tells me this dish goes superbly with a Krönenbourg beer or a semidry Alsatian Riesling.

Necessity really is the mother of invention…and the best recipes. Back in my younger days I whipped this dish up from ingredients I had scrounged from my refrigerator. Have it for breakfast or serve it for lunch with a tossed salad. Very continental!

Mushroom Omelet with Herbes de Provence and Asiago Cheese

2 eggs, beaten

1 teaspoon butter

¼ cup sliced mushrooms

1 tablespoon green onion, chopped

½ teaspoon herbes de Provence
   Salt and pepper

1 teaspoon grated Asiago cheese
   (don't ask me why I had this in my
   fridge at the time…must have been a gift)

1 teaspoon cream cheese, softened

Serves 1

1 In a well-seasoned pan, sauté the mushrooms, onions, and herbes de Provence over medium-high heat in butter until softened. Salt and pepper to taste.

2 Add the eggs to the pan and let the ingredients set. Pull the outer edge of the omelet toward the center of the pan and tilt the pan to let the uncooked egg form a new edge. Add the Asiago cheese and cream cheese to the middle of the omelet. Cover the pan and remove it from the heat to let the eggs set up a bit more.

3 To serve, fold the omelet in the pan once and then once more as you flip it out onto the plate. Garnish with fresh fruit and serve immediately.

Though I love sausage in my lasagna, I've always preferred the bright flavors in
this vegetable lasagna dish. This dish is fantastic with handmade pasta sheets.
At work, I use the frozen fresh variety that you can now buy at the grocery.

Schuler's Signature Lasagna

1   package frozen fresh pasta sheets
1   can crushed tomatoes (24 ounces)
1   can tomato sauce (24 ounces)
    Olive oil
6   cloves garlic, crushed
    Handful of parsley, finely chopped
    Pinch of nutmeg
    Pinch of cinnamon
2   teaspoon fresh basil, chopped
2   teaspoon fresh oregano, chopped
1   ounce butter
1   ounce flour
2 ½ cups milk
1   eggplant, peeled and chopped
2   handfuls fresh spinach
1   small onion
1   zucchini, peeled and chopped
1   carrot, peeled and chopped
1   cup mushrooms, sliced
1   summer squash, chopped
½   pound mozzarella cheese
1   cup grated Parmesan cheese
    Serves 8

1 For the red sauce, heat the olive oil in a medium-sized pot and soften 4 cloves of the garlic and the parsley. Add the crushed tomatoes and the tomato sauce. Stir in the nutmeg and cinnamon and 1 teaspoon each of the basil and oregano. Simmer for 30 minutes and then add the rest of the basil and the oregano. Taste and adjust the seasoning if desired.

2 For the white sauce, melt the butter in a small saucepan and add the flour to make a roux. Cook the roux, whisking regularly, until it smells like popcorn and then add the cold milk. Bring to a boil, and whisk until smooth. Add a dash of nutmeg and salt and pepper to taste.

3 For the filling, sauté the eggplant, spinach, onion, zucchini, carrot, mushroom, and summer squash with 2 cloves of crushed garlic until tender. Salt and pepper to taste.

4 Preheat the oven to 350°.

5 To assemble the lasagna, put some red sauce in the bottom of a greased baking dish. Layer in the following order: pasta sheet, white sauce, vegetables, red sauce, and cheese. Repeat as many times as you can in the dish and top everything with a sprinkle of chopped parsley. Bake until bubbly and golden brown on top, about 1 hour. Let the lasagna rest covered for 15 minutes before cutting to allow it to firm up a bit.

Servers on the kitchen line. Note the time-honored wait staff fashion—
white aprons and collars on black dresses, circa 1970.

This dish is an idea more than a recipe. If you have a garden, visit it in the peak of the late summer harvest to see what you have left and what you need to use. The idea is to avoid making 60 loaves of zucchini bread again this year for all the neighbors and their distant relatives. The "Diablo" comes from the hot peppers that, no doubt, are lurking somewhere in your garden or at the grocery.

Summertime Vegetable Diablo with Angel Hair Pasta

1 each: ear of corn, zucchini, summer squash, tomato, jalapeño pepper, cucumber

Peas

Green beans

Lima beans

Fresh herbs (Do you have lavender? Use it.)

Olive oil

Garlic cloves, crushed

1 tablespoon red wine vinegar

1 pound angel hair pasta

Parmesan cheese (for garnish)

Serves 2–4

1 Bring salted water to a rapid boil in a large pot. Tougher vegetables such as green beans and lima beans need to be partially cooked in the boiling water before they go into the sauté pan. Remove the beans when almost done and reserve with the other vegetables. Keep the water boiling for the pasta.

2 Clean, peel, and chop the vegetables as necessary. In a large skillet, heat the olive oil and soften the garlic. Place all of the vegetables into the pan except for the tomato. Sauté the vegetables until they are tender, and then add the tomato, herbs, and vinegar. Cook a minute more, and salt and pepper to taste.

3 Boil the angel hair pasta until tender, which should only take a minute. Drain the pasta and serve in dinner bowls topped by the Vegetable Diablo and some grated Parmesan cheese for garnish.

I love everything that's old: books and wine. — Goldsmith

Like most of my favorite recipes, this is extremely simple. I make this dish when I have leftover marinara or tomato sauce. Cooking the pasta in the pan with the sauce really infuses the pasta with flavor.

Radiator Pasta with Italian Sausage and Tomato Basil Cream Sauce

2   cups radiator pasta
½   pound ground Italian sausage
1   small onion, chopped fine
2   cloves garlic, crushed
½   cup vodka
1   cup tomato or marinara sauce
½   cup heavy whipping cream
    Fresh basil
    Parmesan cheese
Serves 4

1   Bring a large pot of salted water to a rapid boil. Cook the pasta al dente and drain it under cool running water to stop the cooking process. Set aside.

2   In a sauté pan, brown the Italian sausage over medium-high heat. Add the onion and garlic to the pan and cook until soft (add a dash of olive oil if needed). Remove the pan from the stove and add the vodka. Return to the stove and flame. Cook until the flame dies down.

3   Add the tomato sauce and bring everything to a boil. Stir in the cream and bring back to a boil. Add the pasta to the pan and toss the pasta with the sauce until the pasta is well coated and heated through. Serve in shallow dinner bowls. Garnish with fresh chopped basil and shaved Parmesan cheese.

friends, time,

I came up with this dish as a meatless entrée alternative for a vegetarian friend. We enjoyed it so much that it was dubbed "cookbook worthy." Don't be too constrained by the rules on this recipe. I originally created the sauce by using what vegetables I had on hand and adding them to some tomato sauce I had in my refrigerator.

Fried Eggplant with Boursin Cheese and Sweet Corn Tomato Sauce

| | eggplant, peeled and cut into ½-inch-thick disks (about 8 disks)
¼ cup flour, seasoned with salt and pepper
2 eggs, beaten with a little milk
½ cup fresh bread crumbs
¼ cup grated Parmesan
Olive oil
| red pepper, chopped
| onion, chopped
2 clove garlic, crushed
| small zucchini, chopped
| ear sweet corn, kernels removed
½ cup tomato sauce or tomato concasse
¼ cup cooked black beans
| tablespoon red wine vinegar
| handful of fresh herbs, chopped (basil, oregano, and lavender are favorites)
½ cup Boursin cheese, softened

Serves 2

1 Preheat oven to 350°.

2 Mix the Parmesan cheese and the bread crumbs together. Dredge the eggplant in flour, dip in the egg wash, and cover with the bread crumb/Parmesan cheese mixture. Fry in a skillet with some olive oil until the eggplant is browned on both sides. Remove and place on a baking sheet. Put in the oven to cook all the way through, about 10 minutes.

3 Add the red pepper, onion, garlic, and zucchini to the pan and cook until soft. Add the sweet corn, tomato sauce, black beans, and vinegar and bring the mixture to a boil. Stir in the fresh herbs and cook for a minute longer.

4 To assemble the dish, layer the Boursin cheese between three or four of the eggplant slices. Top with the sauce and garnish with more fresh herbs. This dish goes equally well with a lighter red wine or your favorite white.

Pizza Dough

1 cup warm water (100–110°)
1 package active dry yeast
   Pinch sugar
1 teaspoon salt
1 tablespoon olive oil
3 cups bread flour
   Cornmeal
   Makes 2 medium pizza rounds

1 Place the water in the mixing bowl from your mixer. Sprinkle in the yeast and stir to dissolve. Let everything stand for 5 minutes or until the mixture bubbles.

2 Add the sugar, salt, olive oil, and bread flour to the bowl and knead it with the bread hook attachment for 8–10 minutes at medium speed. The resulting dough should be soft and elastic. Place the dough in an oiled bowl, cover with plastic, and let it rise until it doubles in bulk, about one hour.

3 Punch down the dough and turn out onto a floured surface. Divide the dough into two equal parts, knead it a few minutes, and let it rest for 10 more. Stretch the dough balls into 2 large circles and place them on baking sheets sprinkled with cornmeal. Top as desired and bake in a 450° oven.

Quatro Formaggio Pizza

   Olive oil
1 clove garlic, crushed
1 cup crushed tomatoes
½ teaspoon dried oregano
   Salt and pepper to taste
1 Pizza Dough round
⅔ cup provolone cheese, grated
½ cup fresh ricotta cheese
½ cup soft goat cheese
   (such as Montrachet)
½ cup grated Parmesan
   Serve 2–4

1 Preheat the oven to 450°.

2 Start the sauce by sautéing the garlic in some olive oil. Add the crushed tomatoes and the dried oregano and cook for about 10–15 minutes. Salt and pepper to taste.

3 Spread the sauce over the pizza dough and top with the cheese. I like a calico pattern of provolone, ricotta, and goat cheese with Parmesan sprinkled over the top. If you like, top the pizza with a bit more dried oregano and bake for approximately 15 minutes. Remove when the edges are golden brown and the cheese is bubbling.

Prosciutto Pizza with Pesto and Sun-Dried Tomatoes

1 Pizza Dough round (pg 128)
½ cup pesto
½ cup chicken, diced
1 package prosciutto ham, sliced
¼ cup sun-dried tomatoes
1 cup mozzarella cheese, shredded
Pine nuts for garnish
Fresh basil for garnish
Serves 2–4

1 Preheat oven to 450°.

2 Spread the pesto evenly on the pizza dough. Top with chicken, prosciutto, and sun-dried tomatoes. Cover with the cheese and sprinkle with the pine nuts. Bake in the oven for 15 minutes, or until golden and bubbly. Garnish with thinly sliced basil if desired.

I smoke my own pork shoulder in my smoker with hickory and apple wood. Look for smoked pork at the butcher shop as a suitable alternative.

Smoked Pork Pizza with Barbecue Sauce, Cheddar Cheese, and Scallions

1 Pizza Dough round (pg 128)
½ cup Schuler's BBQ Sauce (pg 26)
⅔ cup smoked pork shoulder, diced
½ cup mozzarella cheese, shredded
½ cup cheddar cheese, shredded
½ cup chopped scallions
Serves 2–4

1 Preheat oven to 450°.

2 Spread the barbecue sauce evenly on the pizza dough. Top with the smoked pork and cover with the mozzarella and the cheddar cheese. Sprinkle the pizza with the scallions and bake for approximately 15 minutes, or until golden and bubbly.

Rotini Noodles with Shrimp, Red Peppers, and Sugar Snap Peas

½ pound dried rotini pasta
    Olive oil
2   cloves garlic
1   red pepper
3   Roma tomatoes, diced
1   pound shrimp, peeled and deveined
1   teaspoon fresh oregano, chopped fine
1½ cup sugar snap peas, blanched
1   tablespoon fresh lemon juice
    Salt and pepper
½   cup crumbled feta cheese for garnish
    Serves 2

1 Cook the pasta in rapidly boiling salted water until done but still firm. Drain and reserve. Blanch the peas in the water and remove.

2 In a medium-hot sauté pan, soften the garlic and red pepper in olive oil. Add the tomatoes, shrimp, and oregano and cook until the shrimp is heated through, but not tough. Squeeze in the lemon juice, add the blanched sugar snap peas and toss. Salt and pepper to taste.

3 Serve the pasta in shallow dinner bowls, cover with the sauce, and sprinkle with the feta cheese. Offer guests a hunk of crusty French bread or toasted pita bread. Serve with a good Mediterranean white wine, such as a high-quality Greek retsina (though some people say retsina is an acquired taste).

Think of this dish as spanakopita without the phyllo dough. This recipe is fantastic with any sort of lamb, and it's also great for a dinner party. Simply mix it up the day before your party and pop it in the oven an hour before your guests arrive.

Crustless Spinach and Cheese Pie

3   eggs, beaten
6   tablespoons flour
2   packages frozen chopped spinach
    (10 ounce), thawed
2   cups cottage cheese (fine curd)
2   cups grated sharp white cheddar cheese
½   teaspoon salt
    Serves 8

1 Preheat oven to 350°.

2 Beat eggs and flour until smooth. Squeeze the water from the thawed spinach. Mix the egg mixture, spinach, cottage cheese, cheddar cheese, and salt together. Pour the mixture into a greased 2-quart casserole. Bake the pie uncovered for one hour or until it puffs in the center and starts to brown on the edges. Let stand 10 minutes before serving.

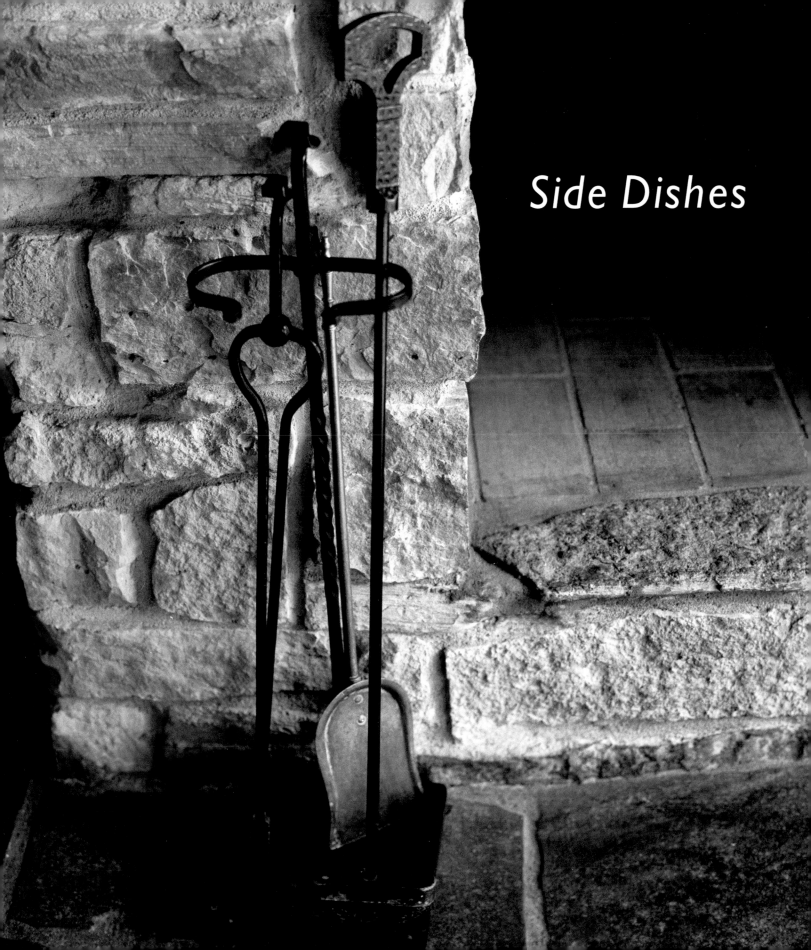

Side Dishes

This particular recipe never fails to please. Its sweetness makes it the perfect accompaniment to pork or wild game. Combined with a crispy potato pancake, this cabbage dish is sure to elicit applause. The color of the cabbage also helps the visual appeal of your side dishes.

Braised Red Cabbage

¼   pound bacon, thick-cut, diced

2   small or 1 large head of red cabbage, trimmed, quartered, and cored

Kosher salt and freshly ground pepper

1   teaspoon caraway seed

1   cup dry red wine

⅓   cup red wine vinegar

3   tablespoons sugar

Serves 8

1 Separate the leaves from the cabbage. Cut away and discard the tough ribs, then cut the cabbage leaves into thin strips.

2 Heat the bacon in a large saucepan or small stockpot over medium-high heat until the bacon renders its fat and begins to brown. Stir regularly so the bacon gets nice and brown without burning or sticking to the bottom of the pan.

3 Add a little of the cabbage at a time with a sprinkle of salt and pepper until the cabbage wilts, and then add some more. Keep up the process until all the cabbage is wilted, then add the caraway seed and cook a minute more. Add the wine and vinegar and bring to a simmer. Stir the sugar over the cabbage and mix well. Reduce the heat to medium-low, partially cover, stirring occasionally, until most of the liquid has evaporated and the cabbage is soft and shiny, about 45 minutes. Remove from the heat and serve.

Ruth Goodrich preparing Schuler's meatballs, circa 1960.

This dish is a traditional accompaniment to prime rib using the melted fat right out of the roasting pan.

Yorkshire Pudding

1   cup plus two tablespoons milk
2   large eggs
1   cup all-purpose flour
1   teaspoon salt
    Freshly ground black pepper to taste
    Serves 12

1   Blend batter in a blender until smooth and transfer to a bowl. Let the batter stand covered for 1 hour. Turn the oven up to 425° after you take out the prime rib.

2   Put a muffin tin on a baking sheet and spoon 1 teaspoon of fat from the roasting pan into each cup. Place the baking sheet into the oven on the middle rack and get the tin and the fat hot. Working quickly, spoon 2 tablespoons of batter into each cup and bake for 15–18 minutes or until the batter is golden and puffed.

This hearty potato dish is a fantastic accompaniment to the French Bistro chicken (pg 111) that's one of my favorites. The richness of the creamy potatoes pairs extremely well with the acidity of the tomato sauce in the chicken dish.

Yukon Gold Smashed Potatoes with Garlic and Chives

2   pounds Yukon Gold potatoes, cleaned but not peeled
½   cup rock salt
3   tablespoons butter
1   teaspoon raw chopped garlic
2   teaspoons finely chopped fresh chives
    Kosher salt and freshly ground pepper to taste
½   cup heavy whipping cream
¾   cup shredded Gruyère cheese
    Serves 8

1   Spread the rock salt out on a baking sheet large enough to hold all of the cleaned potatoes in one layer. Roast the potatoes in the oven at 350° for approximately 40 minutes, or until being tender to the touch. Remove potatoes from the oven and place them in a large bowl to smash, being careful not to get any of the rock salt in your smashing bowl.

2   Smash the potatoes in their skin with the butter, garlic, and chives. Do not whip them smooth or they will lose some of their character. "Lumpy" is acceptable here.

3   Finally, spread the mixture evenly in a greased baking dish and poke a few holes in the skin of the potatoes with your fork. Pour the cream and sprinkle the cheese over the top. Return to the oven and let the potatoes cook 20 additional minutes or until the mixture is bubbly and nicely browned on top.

Roasted Garden Tomatoes

When tomatoes come into season, I eat them many different ways. Not only do they taste great by themselves, but the enzymes and acidity in tomatoes actually brings out the flavor in surrounding foods. That's why you should roast some tomatoes as a garnish for your next meal. Whatever you are making will benefit.

Roasted Garden Tomatoes

Fresh tomatoes
Olive oil
Kosher salt and pepper
Pinch sugar

1 Preheat the oven to 450°.

2 Simply cut off the tops of the ripest tomatoes, drizzle them with olive oil, sprinkle with salt, pepper, and a pinch of sugar, and roast until tender. When done, the tomato should be browning but not quite falling apart. Serve as is or with a dusting of chopped fresh herbs.

Everyone seems to love this dish, and if you have children, even they will ask you to make it again. Baked in a buttered Bundt pan, this becomes a nicely presented dish for a buffet. After you release the ring from the pan, just fill the middle with something green (like buttered peas, for example). For a plated dinner party, bake the mixture in individual buttered ramekins. Turned out onto the plate, the individual disks make a nice presentation.

Festive Carrot Ring

2   cups cooked mashed carrots
1   cup saltine cracker crumbs (28 squares)
1   cup milk
¾   cup shredded sharp cheddar cheese (New York-style extra sharp white cheddar works well)
½   cup soft butter
¼   cup grated onion
1   teaspoon salt
¼   teaspoon pepper
⅛   teaspoon cayenne pepper
3   eggs
     Serves 6

1 Combine all of the ingredients and cook at 350° in a greased Bundt pan, individual ramekins, or a casserole dish until the sides are firm and the top is slightly browned, perhaps 20 minutes for the ramekins and almost twice that for the casserole dish.

This is not technically succotash, but I love the way the name sounds. Like the Summertime Vegetable Diablo with Angel Hair Pasta, this is not as much a recipe as a concept. Visit your garden or the farmer's market and find the freshest, ripest vegetables you can and cook them with some fresh herbs and butter. The result will be fantastic!

Summer Succotash

Any of the following
Sweet corn
Lima beans
Wax beans
Green beans
Peas
Swiss chard
Shallots
Leeks
Zucchini
Carrots
Celery
Any other vegetable I forgot!

1 stick unsalted butter
4 sheets of prosciutto
   Cherry tomatoes
1 handful chopped fresh herbs
   (thyme and chives are excellent)
   Salt and pepper to taste
   Serves 4

I Cook each vegetable in rapidly boiling salted water until tender, but not mushy. Rinse in cold water and combine in a large bowl (cut the kernels from the corn, of course). Discard all but ½ inch of the vegetable water, turn the heat to medium-low, and whisk in the cold butter a little at a time. Add the prosciutto, vegetables, and cherry tomatoes and coat and simmer the mixture with the butter until everything is heated through. Salt and pepper to taste. Serve this dish alone or with the Hazelnut Crusted Walleye and a buttery Chardonnay.

Cheddar Mashed Potatoes

1   pound Yukon Gold potatoes
     Dash of milk
½   cup sour cream
1   tablespoon butter
1   cup sharp white cheddar cheese, grated
     Salt and pepper
     Serves 2–4

I Boil or bake the potatoes, skins on, until tender. In a large bowl, mash the potatoes with a masher and whip in the milk, sour cream, butter, and cheddar cheese. Salt and pepper to taste. Serve immediately.

Roasted Asparagus with Pine Nuts

1   pound asparagus, cleaned with the tough ends cut off

Olive oil

Balsamic vinegar

Salt and pepper to taste

½   cup pine nuts

Serves 4

1 Preheat oven to 400°.

2 In a large bowl, toss the asparagus with enough olive oil, balsamic vinegar, salt, and pepper to coat. Spread on a sheet tray with the pine nuts and roast until the asparagus becomes tender and the pine nuts are brown and toasty, about 10–15 minutes.

Cauliflower with Lemon and Herb Butter

1 pound cauliflower, cleaned and
cut into flowerettes
1 lemon
2 tablespoons Herbed Butter (pg 29)
Salt and pepper to taste
Serves 4

1 With a peeler, remove the zest from the lemon and add to a pot of rapidly boiling salted water. Squeeze the juice from the lemon into the water and add the cauliflower. Cook the cauliflower until it is tender, but not "mushy."

2 In a saucepan, toss the cauliflower with the Herbed Butter over medium-high heat until the cauliflower is heated through. Salt and pepper to taste.

Sautéed Summer Squash with Fresh Mint

1 pound summer squash
Olive oil
2 cloves garlic
1 handful chopped mint
Salt and pepper to taste
Serves 4

1 Wash and cut the summer squash in half, lengthways. Slice into half-moon shapes. Sauté the squash with olive oil, garlic, salt, and pepper until the squash becomes tender. Add the mint and toss the vegetables in the pan to coat. Serve immediately.

The strong, sweet taste of beets stands up well to flavorful items like salmon and wild game.

Balsamic Vinegar Roasted Beets with Marjoram

1 pound beets, peeled and cut
in half through the stems
Olive oil
Balsamic vinegar
Salt and pepper to taste
1 tablespoon fresh marjoram
Serves 4

1 Preheat oven to 400°.

2 In a medium-sized bowl, toss the beets with enough olive oil, balsamic vinegar, salt, and pepper to coat. Add the marjoram and toss.

3 Lay the beets out on a baking sheet and roast until the beets are tender and beginning to wrinkle, about 30 minutes.

Pan Roasted Winter Vegetables

Use any combination of the following
- Beets
- Parsnips
- Rutabagas
- Turnips
- Celery root
- Fennel bulb
- Carrot
- Olive oil

1–2 tablespoons fresh thyme, chopped

½ teaspoon Hungarian paprika

Salt and pepper to taste

Serves 2–4

1 Preheat oven to 400°.

2 Peel and cut the vegetables into similar-sized pieces (keep the beets separate so as not to discolor the other vegetables). In a large bowl, toss the vegetables with olive oil, thyme, paprika, salt, and pepper to coat. Place on a baking sheet and roast until tender, about 30 minutes.

CELEBRATED MEN "Famous Sayings…from the pens of celebrated men are to be found on the beams of Schuler's Restaurant." For those who've visited Schuler's restaurants over the years, the distinctive quotes were conversation pieces that entertained them while they ate. ♦ A key component of the Schuler philosophy is to make the guest comfortable. Figuring that guests like to talk about quotes and comments from celebrities, and drawing upon his love of history and literature, Win came up with the concept of themes for his restaurants. Inscribing quotes on the wooden beams of the buildings also provided a sense of nostalgia for diners. In some instances, instead of British history, contemporary sports figures became the source of the quotes. ♦ And then there was the occasional instance of taking an historical quote and "Schulerizing" it. "Give me a bowl of wine…" appears on the Centennial Room beams in Marshall, and is attributed to Earl Heenan, a Michigan native, war hero, and patron of the restaurant for many years. When a guest who was an English literature professor pointed out that the quote was actually from Shakespeare's *Merchant of Venice*, Win introduced the professor to Earl, who happened to be sitting in the restaurant at the time. With tongue firmly in cheek, Win suggested that Earl was "our modern Shakespeare."

Centennial Room bar, circa 1947.

Try these with the Pan Roasted Duck Breast with Winter Vegetables.
The flavor is phenomenal, and the crisp texture is a nice complement to the tender duck.

Potato Pancakes

2   pounds baking potatoes, peeled
    and held in cold water
1   medium onion, peeled
½   cup chopped scallions
1   egg, beaten
    Salt and fresh ground pepper to taste
    Vegetable oil for frying
    Makes 2 dozen small pancakes

1 Grate the potatoes and the onion. Place in a fine strainer and squeeze out all of the water over a bowl. The potato starch will settle to the bottom of the bowl in a few minutes. Carefully pour off the water and keep the starch. Mix the potato, onion, and starch. Add the egg, scallion, salt, and pepper.

2 Heat the vegetable oil in a heavy skillet. Pat out pancakes (about 2 tablespoons each) and fry in the skillet until golden brown, about 3 minutes on each side. Remove to paper towels to drain. Serve immediately while the pancakes are still hot and crisp.

This, along with the Braised Red Cabbage, belongs with Medallions of Veal with Scallions and White Wine
Sauce. These German dumplings are tender and are great for soaking up any sauce with which they are served.

Spaetzle

1   cup all-purpose flour
½   teaspoon salt
3   large eggs
⅓   cup whole milk
2   tablespoons whole butter
    Serves 2

1 Bring a large pot of salted water to a boil. Fill a large bowl with cold water. Stir together flour and salt. Whisk together eggs and milk, then whisk into the flour until the resulting batter is smooth.

2 Working over the boiling water, force half of the batter through a spaetzle maker or the large holes of a perforated pan (I use the perforated inset of my pasta pot at home). As the dumplings float to the surface, transfer them to the cold water with a slotted spoon. Repeat with the rest of the batter. You can refrigerate the spaetzle for later use if you choose, or finish by tossing them with hot butter in a sauté pan until heated through. Salt and pepper to taste.

Drinks

(Left to right) Jonathan's Soon-to-be-World Famous Margaritas, 1951 Martini, and Saketini

This is nothing like the spiked slush you get at your local Mexican chain restaurant—which is mostly ice and sweet and sour mix. These are more like smooth Mexican Martinis. Beware! They pack a wallop.

Jonathan's Soon-To-Be World Famous Margaritas

1²⁄₃ cup good tequila
(100% blue agave is best!)

¼ cup Grand Marnier or Cointreau

½ cup fresh lime juice (2–3 large limes)

1 teaspoon lime zest, finely grated

6 tablespoons Simple Syrup

Lime wedges

Coarse salt

Serves 8

1 Mix the tequila, orange liqueur, lime juice, lime zest, and Simple Syrup. Cover and refrigerate for at least two hours to allow the flavors to blend.

2 Rub the rim of 8 martini or other 6- to 8-ounce glasses with a lime wedge, then dip the rims in a dish of coarse salt. Put the glasses in the freezer. When chilled, serve the margaritas straight up or over the rocks with a slice of lime for garnish. (Strain the mixture before pouring into the glasses if you don't care for lime zest floating in your drink.)

This is a traditional Cuban drink that is drawing rave reviews in restaurants and bars around the country. Refreshing and different, it will make you think of the islands!

Mojito

4 mint leaves

2½ teaspoons Simple Syrup

1 fresh lime

2 ounces light rum

Crushed ice

Dash of club soda

Serves 1

1 Crush the mint leaves in the bottom of a glass with the simple syrup to release the mint oil. Squeeze the juice from the lime into the glass, pour in the rum, and fill the glass with crushed ice. Finish with a dash of club soda, if you like, and stir. A piece of sugar cane makes a great garnish!

Make as much or as little as you like. It will keep for quite awhile in the refrigerator.

Simple Syrup

1 part water

2 parts sugar

1 Boil for 5 minutes. Store in a tightly-sealed container in the refrigerator.

Whether as a morning libation after a late night of revelry, or as an accompaniment to a Sunday brunch, this longtime favorite should be on everyone's recipe list. Get creative with the garnish and you can have a meal with your drink all in the same glass!

Brunchtime Bloody Mary

3   ounces vodka
6   ounces tomato juice (or V-8)
    Juice from half a lemon
1   teaspoon Worcestershire sauce
4   drops Tabasco sauce
    Dash celery seed
    Salt and fresh ground pepper to taste
Serves 2

1   Stir the ingredients together in a pitcher. Pour into a tall beer glass over ice and garnish with celery, olives, pickles, lemon, cheese, and salami (or any combination thereof).

Champagne Cocktail

4   ounces chilled champagne
1   sugar cube
2   dashes Angostura bitters
    Serves 1

| Place the sugar cube in the bottom of a champagne flute. Soak with the bitters and pour the champagne over the top. Serve with a lemon twist for garnish.

Legend has it that this is the winning recipe from the only World Martini Championship, held at the Drake Hotel in Chicago in 1951. One of the judges was none other than Humphrey Bogart, who taught us that having 2 olives in one's martini is ideal, whereas three is "obscene."

1951 Martini

2   ounces premium gin
½   ounce dry vermouth
    Splash Chambord

| Shaken, not stirred. Served in a chilled martini glass with two anchovy stuffed olives.

I associate this drink with the holidays, and one of these always sounds good while I'm waiting for the prime rib to cook. I usually enjoy it in front of a roaring fire.

My Favorite Manhattan

2   ounces bourbon whiskey
¾   ounce sweet vermouth
3   drops Angostura bitters
    Dash of cherry juice from jar
    Serves 1

| Stir with ice and strain into cocktail glass. Garnish with cherry.

Over the years, Schuler's has become known for pairing fine food with wine. It was the first Michigan restaurant to feature and promote Mondavi wines from California, and some years later, Larry Schuler would work as an intern for Robert Mondavi, learning valuable production and marketing skills associated with that pioneering Napa Valley vintner. ◆ French wines were also featured, beginning as early as the 1960s.

IN VINO VERITAS

The "Great Expectations" wine list of that time listed imported French wines, "California Wines of Distinction," and "An Ankle Breaker of Almaden Rosé," which cost $1 for a quarter liter and $12 for "The Works." ◆ A restaurant review from the 1980s noted that the restaurant was offering a special list of Maison Latour Burgundies "especially chosen by Hans Schuler on a recent trip to France" to mark Schuler's 80th anniversary. ◆ Not all of the wine ended up in the guests. Joe Zangaro,

a former Schuler's bartender, remembered that "once Mr. Schuler (Win) had treated a guest table with a complimentary bottle of Champagne on some special occasion. He opened the bottle with great enthusiasm, and much to his surprise, the champagne foamed out of the bottle and onto the guests. Mr. Schuler's quick reaction was to empty the remaining wine on his own head and declare, 'You are not the only ones treated to a champagne bath'." ◆ Today Schuler's continues to promote fine wine appreciation by sponsoring wine dinners and "Flights of Fancy" wine tasting. "We host several wine dinners throughout the year, and they've proved to be popular, especially because of the pairing of fine wine with food prepared by our fine culinary team," says Hans Schuler.

Michelle Miller selects a special Chardonnay to serve to her Schuler's guests.

Once, at a cooking class, I forgot to put the club soda in this recipe. Recovering quickly, I served the mixture in chilled wine glasses without the ice for what amounted to a Spanish martini.

Party Sangria

2	bottles red wine
I	cup brandy
½	cup Cointreau
2	cups orange juice
I	cup lemon juice
I	cup superfine sugar
	ice cubes
2	cups chilled club soda
I	orange, thinly sliced
I	lemon, thinly sliced

I   Thoroughly chill all ingredients. Pour the wine, brandy, and Cointreau into a large punch bowl. Stir orange and lemon juice with the sugar until sugar has dissolved then add to bowl and stir to blend. Add ice cubes and soda and garnish with fruit slices. Serve in punch glasses or wineglasses.

A great step towards independence is a good= humored stomach.

— Seneca

Brandy Alexander

Brandy Alexander

Real vanilla ice cream
3   ounces brandy
3   ounces crème de cocoa
    Serves 2

1   Fill a blender half full with the vanilla ice cream. Pour in the brandy and the crème de cocoa and blend until smooth. Pour into soda fountain glasses and garnish with whip cream and a sprinkle of nutmeg.

Cosmopolitan

1½ ounces vodka
½   ounce Cointreau
1   ounce cranberry juice
½   ounce fresh lime juice
    Serves 1

1   Combine the ingredients into a shaker over crushed ice. Shake and pour into a chilled martini glass. Garnish with a lime twist.

THE MARSHALL ATHLETIC CLUB Distilled spirits have been an integral part of the Schuler's experience since the restaurant's early days. During an era when prohibition was still a fresh memory and "dry" counties were common, the state liquor commission in Lansing was often choosy when it came to granting liquor licenses. In 1935, after hearing that the "Detroit Athletic Club" had been extremely successful, Win Schuler sought to get a club license for Marshall, which would allow the restaurant to serve liquor in what was then a dry area. When asked what he would call the special area at his restaurant, Win said, "The Marshall Athletic Club." Win's club—30 seats in a small sample room at the Eagle Street location—charged a $2 membership, which was also good toward your first drinks.

Joe Zangaro, Schuler's friendly bartender in full regalia, 1965.

You can make your own simple syrup by boiling 2 parts sugar to 1 part water for 5 minutes.
Add as much as you like to make the Saketini as sweet as you prefer.

Saketini

1	ounce vodka	1	Shaken, not stirred. Served in a
1	ounce sake		chilled martini glass with an orange
½	ounce Cointreau		slice for garnish.
	Splash Blue Curaçao		
	Splash Simple Syrup (or to taste)		

Peach Daiquiri

½	medium fresh peach, pitted and unpeeled	1	Combine all ingredients into
1½	ounces white rum		blender, cover, and process at
½	ounce lime juice		high speed for 10 seconds.
2	teaspoons sugar		
½–1	cup crushed ice		

Serves 1 king-size or 2 regular

THE GUEST SHALL DECIDE Whether it's for the couple celebrating an anniversary, the regular local townspeople, the busload of visitors on a tour of Michigan, or friends throughout the Midwest, Schuler's has always sought to maintain its record of excellent food, service, and hospitality. ♦ The secret to its success may rest with the restaurant's long-standing approach toward its customers. "We have a saying at Schuler's: 'The guest shall decide'," notes Hans Schuler. "By this, we mean that our approaches to everything from the decor to the menu are driven by the needs and opinions of our patrons." ♦ As in Win Schuler's day, the restaurant finds that people are looking for "the nicest place to eat that they can afford." And, whether it is waitresses attired in time-honored white aprons and collars on black dresses, or the continued popularity of longtime Schuler's favorites such as prime rib, guests continue to make decisions that help Schuler's remain the quintessential Midwestern restaurant with many of the characteristics that put it on the map in the first place.

Hans Schuler greets the Kevin and Patty Belew family from Marshall, with daughters Kate and Grace and son Aidan.

Desserts

Chocolate Bread Pudding with Coffee Liqueur

6   slices firm white bread
    (like Jewish challah)

1   cup whole milk

1   whole vanilla bean

2   beaten eggs

1   cup sugar

½   cup cocoa

½   cup almond slivers

2   ounces Kahlúa

Serves 6

1 Toast the almonds in the oven on a baking sheet for 5–10 minutes, or until light brown. Remove and set aside. Remove the crust and cube the bread. Reserve in a stainless steel bowl. Scrape out the insides of vanilla bean and add with the husk to milk in a saucepan. Scald the mixture and pour over bread cubes in a bowl.

2 Whisk together the sugar and cocoa in another bowl and then whisk in the eggs until a chocolate paste is formed. Add the chocolate mixture to the bread and combine with a spatula until all signs of the white disappear.

3 Pour the mixture in buttered casserole and bake in a water bath for 40–45 minutes at 350°.

4 Spoon individual servings of the pudding onto 6 different dessert plates, drizzle with a small amount of Kahlúa, and top with whipped cream and toasted almonds.

Grandma's Pie Crust

⅔ cup lard
2 tablespoons butter
2 cups all-purpose flour
1 teaspoon salt
¼ cup (approximate) ice cold water
**Makes 2 nine-inch pie shells
or 1 pie**

1 Sift the flour and salt together in a large bowl. Cut the lard and butter into the flour using your hands or a cutter until the fat pieces are the size of peas.

2 Add the water gradually, gently mixing with your hands until the dough holds together. Do not overmix or the crust will be tough. Cover the dough with plastic wrap and chill before using.

Key Lime Pie

For pastry shell
Grandma's Pie Crust recipe
Pie weights or raw rice for weighting shell

For filling
1 pound cream cheese, softened
¾ cup fresh lime juice
1 14-ounce can sweetened condensed milk
1 teaspoon finely grated fresh lime zest
1 cup crème fraiche
¼ cup confectioners' sugar
8 lime slices for garnish
Serves 8

Make crust

1 On a lightly floured surface, roll out half of Grandma's dough (save the other half for another use) into a 15-inch round (about ⅛-inch thick) and fit into a 9-inch (1 quart) glass pie plate. Trim the dough, leaving a ½-inch overhang, and crimp the edge. Prick the shell all over with a fork. Chill the shell for 30 minutes.

2 Preheat oven to 350°.

3 Line the shell with foil and fill it with pie weights or raw rice. Bake the shell in the lower third of the oven for 20 minutes. Carefully remove foil and weights (or rice) and bake the shell until golden brown, about 10–15 minutes more. Cool the shell completely on a rack.

Make filling

4 In a food processor, blend the cream cheese, lime juice, and condensed milk until smooth. Add the zest and pulse just long enough to combine. Pour the filling into the shell. In a bowl with an electric mixer, beat crème fraiche with confectioners' sugar until it forms soft peaks and spreads evenly over the filling. Arrange the lime slices on top of the pie. Chill the pie, loosely covered, at least 6 hours and up to 1 day.

Coconut Snowball

My daughter, Jessica, once made a special trip from Western Michigan University in
Kalamazoo to Marshall just for this dessert. As you can tell, she has a serious sweet tooth.

Coconut Snowball

Real vanilla ice cream
½ cup coconut flakes
Fudge sauce
Serves 1

1 Preheat the oven to 350°.

2 Toast the coconut flakes on a baking sheet in the oven for about 10 minutes, or until the coconut is toasty brown. Remove from oven and allow the coconut to cool. Heat the fudge sauce in a saucepan.

3 Depending on your appetite, fashion a small (or not so small) ball of vanilla ice cream with your ice cream scoop and roll it in the toasted coconut. Ladle some hot fudge onto a plate or into a shallow bowl and top with the snowball. Garnish with a strawberry and some fresh mint and serve immediately.

Try these cookies. They are easy to make, and are a novelty because you leave
them in the oven overnight (kids think this is cool), and they are melt-in-your
mouth delicious. I love all types of cookies, but these are my all-time favorite.

Nighty-Night Cookies

3   egg whites
½ teaspoon cream of tartar
1   cup sugar
1½ cups chocolate chips
1½ cups pecan pieces
Makes 2 dozen

1 Preheat to 350°.

2 Beat the egg whites and the cream of tartar with the wire whisk attachment on your mixer until soft peaks are formed. Add the sugar slowly and keep whipping until stiff peaks are formed. Fold in the chocolate chips and pecan pieces.

3 Using a tablespoon, spoon out and drop the cookie dough onto a foil-lined baking sheet. The cookies should have a peak almost like a big Hershey's Kiss. Transfer the cookies to the oven and turn off the oven. Leave overnight. The cookies will be done in the morning.

My mom used to leave a sign on the oven so we would not open the door and let the heat out. This might be a good idea if you have curious little people around the house.

Lemon Dream Bars with Raspberry Coulis

Crust

½ cup butter
1 cup flour
¼ cup powdered sugar
⅛ teaspoon salt

Filling

2 tablespoons flour
1 cup sugar
½ teaspoon baking powder
⅛ teaspoon salt
2 eggs beaten
½ cup fresh lemon juice

Frosting

½ cup powdered sugar
1 tablespoon lemon juice
1 tablespoon melted butter
Serves 12

Crust

1 Mix the ingredients together as you would a pie crust and pat into an 8 x 11 inch pan. Bake for 20 minutes at 350°.

Filling

2 Sift flour, sugar, baking powder, and salt together. Add to the beaten eggs and lemon juice. Pour the mixture into the crust and bake for 25 minutes at 350°.

Frosting

3 Add the sugar to the lemon juice and butter and mix until smooth. Drizzle the frosting over the filling after the bars have come out of the oven.

Raspberry Coulis

2 quarts raspberries
½ cup sugar
¼ cup raspberry jam

1 Blend all ingredients in a food processor and strain. Chill in refrigerator before serving.

It was hard to select a cheesecake for this book because I have tried so many variations that have all been good. It's cheesecake, after all! This one has stood out for everyone who has tried it. The only complaint I've ever had is that someone said the coffee in it kept them up after they enjoyed a piece for a late-night snack. The next time I made it with decaf.

Coffee Cheesecake

8   whole graham crackers
6   tablespoons melted butter
4   8-ounce packages cream cheese
1½ cup sugar
4   eggs
2   tablespoons flour
½   cup whipping cream
4   teaspoons finely ground coffee
2   teaspoons vanilla extract
    Whipped cream
    Chocolate chips, curls, or fans for garnish
    Chocolate sauce
    Serves 12

1 Preheat oven to 350°.

2 In a food processor, mix the graham crackers, butter, and ¼ cup sugar until well blended. Remove the mix and pat it into the bottom of a 9-inch springform pan to form a crust. Bake the crust for 10 minutes in the oven to set. Remove and grease the inside walls of the pan.

3 In your mixer, beat the cream cheese with your paddle attachment until smooth. While your mixer is still running, gradually add the remaining 1¼ cup sugar and then the eggs, one at a time. Add the flour, whipped cream, coffee, and vanilla and continue to beat until the batter is well blended. You may have to scrape down the sides a time or two to incorporate everything equally.

4 Pour the batter into the greased springform pan and bake for about one hour, or until the cake is puffed and cracking and the center is just beginning to set. Remove and refrigerate uncovered until cake is chilled through, about 4–6 hours.

5 Spoon chocolate sauce onto a plate and place a piece of the cheesecake on top. Garnish with chocolate chips and whipped cream.

Grasshopper Pie {PHOTO PG 9}

2 cups Oreo cookie crumbs
¾ stick unsalted butter, melted
⅓ cup milk
⅓ pound miniature marshmallows
1½ ounce green crème de menthe
1½ ounce white crème de cocoa
1⅓ cup whipping cream
 Chocolate sauce
 Serves 6

1 Preheat oven to 350°. Stir Oreo crumbs and butter together until ingredients are moist. Press into the bottom of a 9-inch pie pan. Bake for 12 minutes. Remove and cool.

2 In a double boiler, heat the milk and the marshmallows until melted. Set aside to cool.

3 Whip the cream. Add the crème de menthe and the crème de cocoa and continue to whip until stiff. Fold the whipped cream into the cooled marshmallow mixture and pour into the crust. Freeze for at least 2 hours.

3 Put chocolate sauce onto a plate and place a piece of the pie on top of the sauce. Garnish with a little whipped cream and a strawberry.

You don't need an ice cream maker for this recipe. It can be made with a bread pan. The richness of real ice cream will surprise and delight you!

Malted Ice Cream

5 ounces sugar
5 eggs
5 ounces malt powder
1 teaspoon vanilla extract
2 cups heavy whipping cream
 Pecans
 Serves 8

1 Whip together the sugar, eggs, and vanilla over hot water until the sugar is dissolved and the mixture is warm to the touch. Whip in malt powder until smooth.

2 In another bowl, whip heavy cream until soft and fold the sugar and egg mixture into the whipped cream.

3 Line a bread pan with plastic wrap, add a layer of crushed pecans and pour in the ice cream mixture. Freeze until solid, about 4 hours, and slice to serve. Serve with chocolate sauce if desired.

If there is one thing we know how to do here in Michigan, it's how to make handmade fruit pies.
This is my favorite, and I know it was my grandfather's favorite, too.

Strawberry Rhubarb Pie

Grandma's Pie Crust (pg 155)

2   cups rhubarb, chopped

2   cups strawberries, stemmed and sliced

1⅓ cup sugar

⅓   cup flour

2   tablespoons butter

Serves 6

1 Preheat the oven to 400°.

2 Divide Grandma's Pie Crust dough in half and roll out each half on a floured surface. Make sure each is big enough to hang over the edge of a 9-inch pie pan. Line the bottom of the pan with the first half.

3 In a large bowl, combine the rhubarb, strawberries, sugar, and flour. Mix together and empty into the pie shell. Dot the top of the filling with the butter. Place the second pie crust over the top.

4 Cut away the extra dough from the edge of the pan, leaving about ¾ inch of both crusts hanging over the edge. Fold the two crusts together and crimp to seal. Cut vents of your own design in the top of the crust and sprinkle with sugar. Cover your crimping with aluminum foil to prevent overbrowning. Bake for about one hour or until the filling starts to bubble out of the vents and the crust is a golden brown. Let the pie cool on a wire rack until ready to serve. I like mine with a scoop of vanilla ice cream.

Peppermint Ribbon Pie

2   cups Oreo cookie crumbs

¾   stick unsalted butter, melted

2   pints peppermint ice cream, slightly softened

I   cup fudge

4   egg whites

½   teaspoon cream of tartar

½   cup sugar

    Chocolate sauce

Serves 6

1 Preheat oven to 350°. Stir Oreo crumbs and butter together until ingredients are moist. Press into the bottom of a 9-inch pie pan. Bake for 12 minutes. Remove and cool.

2 Spread out one pint of the peppermint ice cream in the chocolate pie crust. Pour the fudge over the ice cream and spread with a spatula. Spread the second pint over the fudge. The fudge should be a "ribbon" between the two layers of ice cream. Freeze for a couple of hours until the ice cream is hard again.

3 Preheat the oven to 350°.

4 Whip the egg whites with the cream of tartar until soft peaks are formed. Add the sugar and continue to whip until the whites are still. Scoop and spread the meringue over the top of the pie with a spatula, forming peaks in the meringue as you finish. Bake for 15 minutes, or until the meringue sets and is starting to brown. Remove and place back in freezer. Let the pie set for 2 more hours.

5 Slice and serve with chocolate sauce and a peppermint stick for garnish.

Peanut Butter Pie

¾   cup graham cracker crumbs

I   cup sugar

2   tablespoons (packed) golden brown sugar

¼   cup (½ stick) unsalted butter, melted

I   8-ounce package cream cheese, room temperature

I   cup creamy peanut butter (do not use old-fashioned kind or freshly ground)

I   tablespoon vanilla extract

1½   cups chilled whipping cream

    Purchased hot fudge sauce

Serves 8

1 Mix graham cracker crumbs, ¼ cup sugar, and brown sugar in medium bowl. Add butter and stir until blended. Press the mixture onto the bottom and up the sides of a 9-inch-diameter glass pie pan. Refrigerate while preparing the filling.

2 Beat the cream cheese, peanut butter, vanilla, and remaining ¾ cup of sugar in a large bowl until smooth. Using an electric mixer with clean, dry beaters, beat the cream in another large bowl until stiff peaks form. Gently fold the whipped cream into the peanut butter mixture in 4 additions. Spoon the filling into the prepared crust, mounding it in the center. Freeze until firm, about 2 hours. This recipe can be prepared one day ahead. Cover and keep frozen. If desired, warm the hot fudge sauce according to directions on the container. Cut the pie into wedges. Serve with the hot fudge sauce.

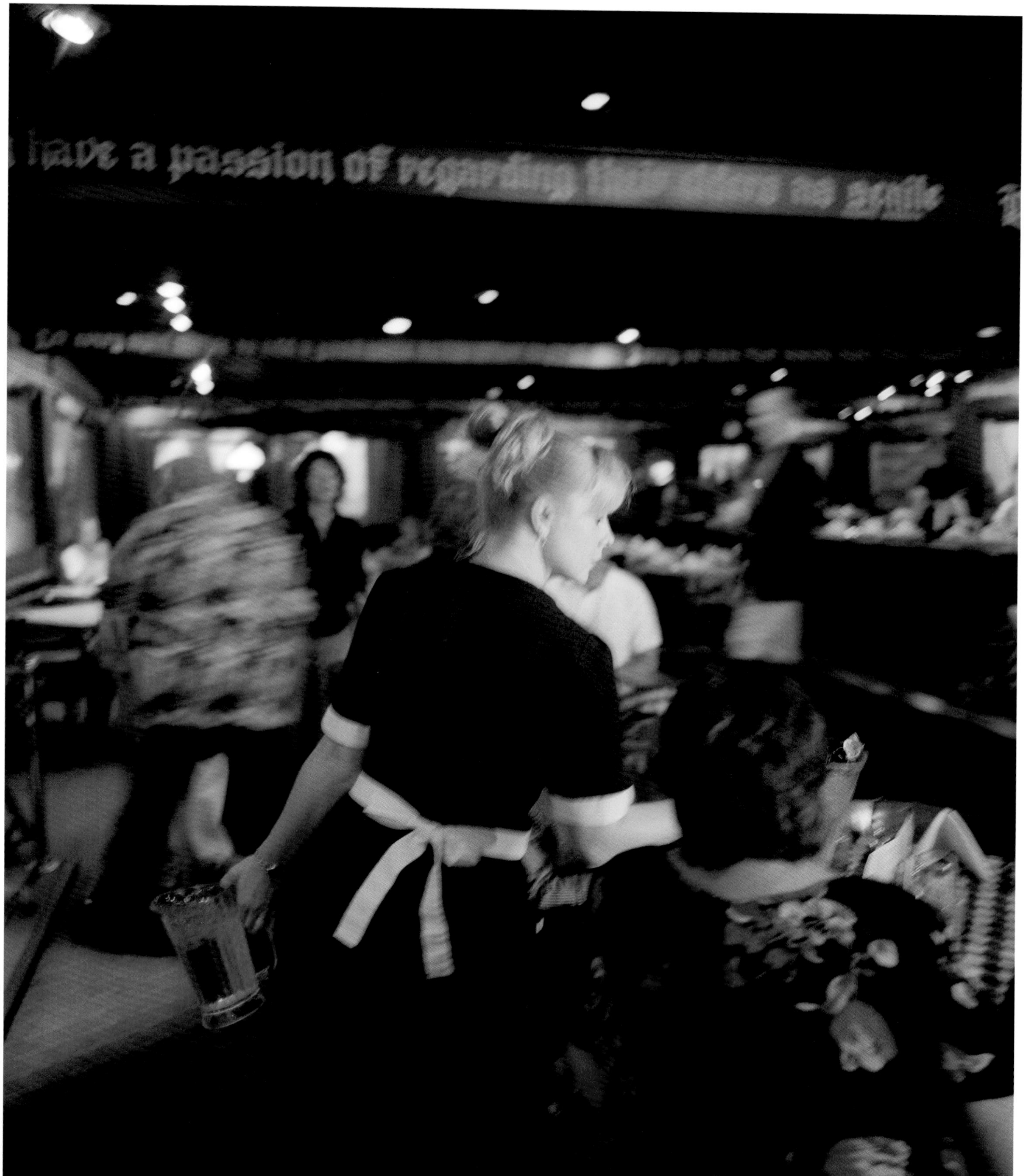
have a passion of regarding

Schuler's guests continue to come from far and wide to dine at the restaurant, and their loyalty is legendary. Over the years, guest comment cards have included entries from throughout the region—Detroit, Toledo, Troy, Jackson, Lansing, Kalamazoo, Ft. Wayne, and, of course "home-towners" from Marshall and nearby Battle Creek, but other visitors hailed from states such as California, Maryland, Kentucky, Minnesota, and Alabama. Schuler's appeal continues to be national and even international—with today's guests coming from as far away as Canada, China, Germany, England, and Japan. ◆ Some are lured by the restaurant's reputation passed along by loved ones over the years. "My father used to stop here," noted a guest from Ohio. Others are longtime customers. "I celebrated my 12th birthday here in 1957," wrote one, "and we have come back here many times for family celebrations since then." Another guest wrote, "We have come here for years, since we were children." Other guests simply appreciate the exceptional service and food that remain hallmarks of Schuler's.

"Great waitress," "Still love your cheese," and "The fish was superb," are examples of kudos offered by happy diners. ◆ No matter what the reason given, it's clear that this is no ordinary restaurant to its guests. One hyperbolic visitor exclaimed, "This remains the best place to eat on Earth." Whether or not that is literally the case, it's the thought that counts. ◆ A new generation of fans is

"THIS REMAINS THE BEST PLACE TO EAT ON EARTH"

also finding Schuler's. "First time at your restaurant; great food, great service!" is a typical entry. That kind of connection is what Schuler's strives to achieve with all of its guests. ◆ "At Schuler's we are really in the relationship business. Our guests know what to expect. From families that spend holiday dinners with us, to busloads of visitors from across the Midwest, to the local business person who wants a quiet lunch or dinner in the restaurant or the pub, our guests all have stories to tell, and we consider them part of the Schuler family," says Hans Schuler.

Cyndi Adkins makes sure that guests' water glasses are refilled.

Baked Michigan Apples with Homemade Caramel Sauce

8   firm and tart apples
    (Granny Smith or
    Northern Spy work well)

2   cups brown sugar

1   stick butter

1   cup pecan pieces

    Serves 8

1 Preheat the oven to 350°.

2 Core the apples and peel the skins
off the top third of the fruit. Line
the apples in a baking pan and stuff
the insides with the brown sugar,
butter, and pecan pieces. Make sure
you have enough filling to mound
the apples high. Bake for about 30
minutes, basting the apples occasionally with the caramel melting in
the pan, until the apples are tender
and just starting to split.

3 Serve individual apples on a plate
drizzled with sauce from the pan
and a fresh scoop of vanilla ice
cream. Garnish with a mint leaf.

This dish is best served nice and warm. Time it so that you bake the topping when
your family sits down to eat. The crisp will be done when you are ready for dessert.

Michigan Apple Crisp

1½ pounds baking apples, peeled and sliced
   (Michigan Granny Smith or
   Northern Spy)

¼ cup brown sugar

1 teaspoon ground cinnamon

⅛ teaspoon nutmeg

⅛ teaspoon salt

2 teaspoons fresh lemon juice

1 tablespoon unsalted butter

Topping

1½ cup brown sugar

½ cup rolled oats

½ cup walnut pieces

   Pinch salt

¾ teaspoon ground cinnamon

½ cup flour

¼ cup unsalted butter

¾ teaspoon vanilla extract

Serves 6 to 8

1 Preheat the oven to 450°.

2 Toss the apples, brown sugar, cinnamon, nutmeg, salt, and lemon juice in a bowl to combine. Let everything stand for 30 minutes to allow the apple mixture to become juicy. Pour into a 9-inch pie pan and dot with the butter. Bake for 30 minutes covered in foil that has a vent cut in the middle to allow the steam to escape.

3 In a large bowl, stir together the brown sugar, oats, walnut pieces, salt, cinnamon, and flour. Fold in the butter using a pastry cutter or your hands until the mixture resembles coarse meal. Pinch some of the topping together to form small clumps.

4 Remove the foil from the apples, cover with the topping, and bake for 30 additional minutes. Serve with a scoop of vanilla or caramel ice cream.

Chocolate Meringue with Fresh Raspberries and Whipped Cream

Chocolate Meringue with Fresh Raspberries and Whipped Cream

6   egg whites
1   teaspoon cream of tartar
1   cup sugar
3   tablespoons unsweetened
    Hershey's cocoa powder
1   teaspoon Chambord
1   cup chocolate chips

2   cups whipping cream
4   tablespoons sugar
1½ pint raspberries
    Serves 8

1 Preheat the oven to 350°.

2 Beat the egg whites and cream of tartar until smooth peaks form. Beat in the sugar until the peaks become stiff and shiny. Fold in the cocoa powder, Chambord and chocolate chips until thoroughly mixed. Spoon the mixture out onto a foil-lined baking sheet to form a pie-sized meringue cookie. Place in the oven and turn the temperature down to 300°. Bake for about one hour or until the edges start to crack, but the meringue doesn't look too dried out. Remove from the oven and cool.

3 Sweeten the raspberries with the sugar and spoon them over the meringue cookie. Top with the whipped cream and drizzle with a little more Chambord. Or, if you want something a bit more decorative, arrange the berries on top of the whip cream as in the photo. Slice and serve at the table.

Chocolate Silk Pie

2   cups graham cracker crumbs
    (about 10 crackers)
¾   stick unsalted butter, melted
⅓   cup sugar

6   ounces bittersweet chocolate, chopped
4   ounces unsweetened chocolate, chopped
1   cup sugar
½   cup cornstarch
¾   teaspoon salt
6   large egg yolks
4½ cups milk
3   tablespoons unsalted butter, softened
1½ teaspoon vanilla extract

1   cup heavy cream
2   tablespoons sugar
    Chocolate curls for garnish
    Serves 6

1 Preheat oven to 350°.

2 Stir together the graham cracker crumbs, unsalted butter, and sugar until the ingredients are moist. Press into the bottom of a 9-inch pie tin. Bake for 12 minutes. Remove and cool.

3 In a double boiler, melt the chocolate until it is smooth. In a saucepan, whisk together the sugar, cornstarch, salt, and egg yolks. Whisk in the milk in a steady stream and bring to a boil over medium heat. Whisk and simmer until thick, about one minute. Transfer the custard to a bowl.

4 Whisk the melted chocolate into the custard mixture with the butter and vanilla until smooth. Cover and cool in the refrigerator. Pour filling into the crust and chill at least 6 more hours.

5 Whip the cream and sweeten with the sugar. Spoon whipped cream decoratively on the pie and sprinkle with chocolate shavings.

I've never served this to a family member who has not been skeptical. "Vinegar?" "For dessert?"
It's just as good as traditional strawberry shortcake, however…with a bright, bold twist.

Strawberry Shortcake with Balsamic Vinegar Reduction

2   cups flour

1/3   cup sugar

1   tablespoon baking powder

1/2   teaspoon salt

1/2   cup unsalted butter, cut into pieces and chilled

1   egg, beaten

1/2   cup whole milk

    Melted butter for brushing

2   pints strawberries, washed, stemmed, and sliced

1   cup balsamic vinegar (I recommend the version from Modeno, Italy)

    Sugar to taste

1   cup heavy whipping cream

2   tablespoons sugar

Serves 6

1   Sift together the flour, sugar, baking powder, and salt. Fold in the chilled butter using your fingers or a pastry cutter until it resembles coarse meal. Add the milk and egg and mix only until incorporated. Chill, covered, for 30 minutes.

2   Preheat oven to 350°.

3   In a saucepan, boil the balsamic vinegar until it is reduced by half. It should be thick enough to coat the back of a spoon. Taste and add a little sugar if desired. Pour over the strawberries and let them steep while shortcake bakes.

4   Roll out the dough on a floured surface to a thickness of 1 inch. Cut the dough into 2½-inch squares and bake until golden brown, about 15 minutes. Remove and brush with melted butter.

5   Whip the cream and sweeten with the sugar. Place a shortcake on a dessert plate and spoon the strawberry mixture over the shortcake. Top with another shortcake. Dollop with whipped cream and garnish with a mint leaf.

The difference between good just a little extra effort.

— Biggie Munn

Some of the world's greatest berries are grown just down the road from Schuler's. If you live in the Midwest (or have similar berry farms in your region), it makes for a fun day to try one of the many "U-Pick 'Em" farms and make a good cobbler out of your efforts. I have added a little cinnamon and nutmeg to the original recipe. I think you will like the results.

South Haven Blueberry Cobbler

½ cup sugar

1 teaspoon cornstarch

4 cups fresh blueberries

1 teaspoon lemon juice

½ teaspoon ground cinnamon

¼ teaspoon ground nutmeg

Topping

½ cup flour

1 tablespoon sugar

1 teaspoon baking powder

1 large egg

3 tablespoons melted butter

¼ cup heavy cream

Serves 6

1 Preheat oven to 400°.

2 Combine the sugar and cornstarch in a bowl. Blend in the blueberries, lemon juice, cinnamon, and nutmeg. Empty into a 2-quart casserole dish and set aside.

3 For the topping, combine the flour, sugar, and baking powder in a bowl. In another bowl, whisk the egg, melted butter, and cream. Mix the wet and dry ingredients together until just combined. Do not over-mix. Drop the dough in spoonfuls over the blueberries, spreading evenly over the surface. Bake about 30 minutes, or until the topping is golden brown. Serve warm with vanilla ice cream.

and great is

Jonathan and Hans Schuler

Back to the Future

In this day and age, it's been said that the greatest challenge for a restaurant is to change with the times, and any successful establishment has had to develop long-range plans addressing changing eating habits and lifestyles. The extraordinary thing is that Schuler's has been doing that for a long, long time.

As a result, today we have a different culture and mind-set than most restaurants. In an age of "cookie-cutter" chains, food courts, and impersonal eateries, we understand that the bottom line continues to be our guests. Our goal is to always provide something new, something fresh, whether it is bread from our bakeshop or new menu items. We understand our customers, and continue to evolve and change to serve them better, while respecting our heritage and the basics of Midwestern cuisine.

I'm certainly proud of what we've accomplished over the years. Reputation, like success in business, is a challenge to maintain. What succeeds in the short term is often more difficult to sustain over the long haul. Good will *has to be renewed* to be lasting.

Being true to what you do best is one part of providing a superior dining experience. Always looking to improve the menu and the decor is another. Providing exceptional hospitality in impersonal times is also essential. In all of these areas, the greatest competition we have is ourselves. Our continuing challenge is to do the little things that keep bringing people back. Dad saw the value of keeping our customers happy. "We always remember to treat these good folks as VIPs: Very Important Pocketbooks," he'd say. But he also saw our guests as something more—friends and family—and we still do today.

As we approach another milestone for the family and the restaurant, I take heart in the fact that we've been able to build on what my grandfather began so many years ago. I'm proud that my son Jonathan has embraced our family's love of cooking and has the skills to match. We hope that you'll have many hours of enjoyment resulting from the recipes Jon's crafted for you here.

As a restaurant owner, following the steps of my father and grandfather, and with more than four decades of experience, I still love to get up in the morning and come to work. I am committed to exceeding the expectations of our guests, and I hope to be looking for you at Schuler's for many years to come.

As I look back on the experiences of four generations in our family, we'll do well to keep in mind that merely staying in business for many years isn't nearly as important as keeping an open mind, evolving, and continuing to improve on what we do—with help from friends like you. Here at Schuler's, we'd like to think that, in some small way, we've managed to do just that.

— *Hans Schuler*

Clara Stewart, Hans Schuler, Ali Webb, Joe Stewart, and Keith Kehlbeck

Acknowledgments

I am extremely pleased to acknowledge the contributions of individuals who took an interest in this book and who made the final product possible.

An unsung hero is our Vice President and General Manager Sue Damron. She keeps things running smoothly at the restaurant on a daily basis, and routinely displays a professionalism that does credit to the Schuler's tradition. This was particularly true during the time we worked on the book, and her presence made that process much easier than it would have been otherwise.

Shondel Neal deserves special praise as project manager and for keeping us all on task during the editorial cycle—no mean feat, I assure you. Her patience, perseverance, and organizational skills helped immensely with the project.

Schuler's Executive Chef, Bill Scott, whose low-key and selfless demeanor masks an instinctive talent in the kitchen, continues to build on the restaurant's high culinary standards, and worked closely with Jonathan to bring these recipes to the printed page.

Keith Kehlbeck spent many hours pouring over archival material and captured the rich history of our family through his exceptional writing. He is a friend, author, historian, and wine lover extraordinaire, and I deeply appreciate his taking time from his busy professional life to write and edit the copy for this book.

My family has been supportive throughout this process. My wife, Nancy, has shared her usual insightful thoughts and perspective on the book, along with her encouragement. Obviously, I'm extremely proud of our "fourth generation," my sons Larry and Jonathan, and daughters Suzanne and Elizabeth.

In particular, it was a marvelous experience to work with Jon, whose love for the food business and *joie de vivre* comes through clearly in his recipes.

Finally, I would be remiss if I didn't acknowledge those without whom there would be no Schuler's—our guests. In many ways, this book is for you; use it in good health as you reminisce and create dishes for *your* friends and families.

— *Hans Schuler*

Special Thanks from the Chef

Thank you to my team, who gave generously of their time and talents to test these recipes: Frank Baker, Sandy Bohnet, Jari Davison, Jill Miller, Elizabeth Schuler, and Suzanne Schuler Wilcox.

A special thanks to Kent and Jennifer Whistler, whose constant support and encouragement were instrumental in completing this project, and to my mom, Nancy Barnhart, whose loving influence was never far from my mind.

Finally, I'd like to thank my beautiful daughters, Jessica and Jordan, these pages are for you.

— *Jonathan Schuler*

For 95 years, the Schuler's tradition has attracted new generations of customers, like Kate Belew of Marshall

Index

1951 Martini 145

aioli, Garlic and Herb 30
anchovy 56
appetizers and hors d'oeuvres 43–58
apples
    Baked Michigan Apples with
        Homemade Caramel Sauce 166
    cider 114
    juice 115
    Michigan Apple Crisp 167
artichoke
    Artichoke and Crab Stuffed
        Mushroom Caps *44*, 45
    Baked Artichoke Hearts 56
arugula 49, 68
Asiago cheese 122
asparagus
    Roasted Asparagus with Pine Nuts 137
    Tortellini a la Crème with Ham and
        Mushrooms 121
au jus 70, 107
avocado
    Avocado Sweet Potato Vichyssoise 76
    Seviche and Avocado Salad 42

bacon
    Bitter Green Salad with Sweet
        Potatoes, Bacon, and Oranges *40*, 41
    Braised Red Cabbage 132
    Midwestern Corn Chowder 73
    Pâté du Maison 50
    Quiche Lorraine 120
    Schuler's Seafood Chowder 74
Baked Artichoke Hearts with Bread
    Crumbs and Fresh Herbs 56
Baked Michigan Apples with Homemade
    Caramel Sauce 166
Baked Potato Soup 77
Balsamic Vinaigrette 39

balsamic vinegar
    Balsamic Vinaigrette 39
    Strawberry Shortcake and Balsamic
        Vinegar Reduction 170
    Balsamic Vinegar Roasted Beets with
        Marjoram 138
barbecue
    Dry Barbeque Rub 25
    Jonathan's Barbecued Baby Back Ribs
        114
    Schuler's BBQ Sauce 26
    Smoked Pork Pizza 129
Bar-Scheeze 22
basil
    Basil Pesto 27
    Fresh Basil, Tomato and Camembert
        on Grilled Sourdough 66
    Savory Pesto Cheesecake 55
    Tomato Basil Cream Sauce 125
beans
    garbanzo 47
    Great Northern 104
    lima beans 82, 104
    navy beans 82
    pinto beans 82
    red kidney beans 82
beef
    Beef Carpaccio and Arugula with
        Lemon Herb Vinaigrette 49
    Beef Short Ribs Braised in Red Wine
        102
    Filet of Beef with a Cognac
        Peppercorn Sauce 109
    French Dip 70
    Grandma Schuler's Cornish Pasties
        103
    Hot Beef Brisket Sandwich 64
    London Broil 115
    New England Pot Roast 115
    Prime Rib Sandwich with Sweet Onion
        Relish and Maytag Blue Cheese 68
    Schuler's Classic Reuben Sandwich 62
    Schuler's Famous Meatballs 46
    Schuler's Famous Prime Rib 107

Beef Stock 24
beer 73
beer cheese 22
beets, roasted 91, 138
bisque
    Mushroom 80
    Pumpkin 80
Bitter Green Salad with Sweet Potatoes,
    Bacon, and Oranges *40*, 41
Blackened Perch with Spicy Remoulade
    Sauce 84
black-eyed peas 82
Bloody Mary 144
blueberries 171
bourbon 145
Boursin cheese 127
Braised Red Cabbage 132
brandy 93, 148, 151
Brandy Alexander *150*, 151
bread pudding, chocolate 154
breads
    Jalapeño Corn Bread 58
    Herbed Focaccia 53
Brigadoon Salad 32, *33*
Brunchtime Bloody Mary 144
butter, herbed 29
button mushrooms 115

cabbage
    Braised Red Cabbage 132
    Schuler's Famous Cole Slaw 37
Camembert cheese 66
Cantaloupe and Prosciutto with Mixed
    Greens, Mint, and Mozzarella 41
capers 56
caramel sauce 166
carrots
    Beef Short Ribs Braised in Red Wine
        102
    Festive Carrot Ring 135
    Michigan Bean and Vegetable Soup 82
    Pan Roasted Duck Breast with Winter
        Vegetables 118

Pan Roasted Winter Vegetables 139
    Schuler's Signature Lasagna 123
    Summer Succotash 136
Cassoulet of Sausages 104
Cauliflower with Lemon and Herb
    Butter 138
Center Cut Pork Chops with a Dijon
    Cream Sauce 100
Champagne Cocktail 145
cheddar cheese
    Baked Potato Soup 77
    Cheddar Mashed Potatoes 136
    Crustless Spinach and Cheese Pie 130
    Festive Carrot Ring 135
    Michigan Country Apple Salad with
        Cheddar Cheese and Croutons 35
    Prosciutto Cheese Straws 48
    Schuler's Heritage Cheese Spread 47
cheese
    Asiago 122
    beer cheese 22
    Boursin 127
    Camembert 66
    cottage 130
    cream 48, 155, 160, 163
    goat 48, 128
    gouda 64
    Gruyère 70, 73, 133
    Maytag blue 68
    mozzarella 41, 123, 129
    ricotta 128
    provolone 128
    Swiss 62, 120
    See also cheddar cheese, Parmesan
        cheese
cheese straws 48
cheesecake
    Coffee 160
    Savory Pesto 55
cherries 108
chickpeas 61, 79
chicken
    Chicken and Arugula Sandwich on
        Focaccia 68

Curried Chicken Salad with Fresh
   Fruit and Walnuts 32
French Bistro Chicken with Tarragon
   Tomato Sauce *110*, 111
Marinated Breast of Chicken Dakota
   101
Mediterranean Roast Chicken with
   Pan Braised Potatoes 105
Pâté du Maison 50
Seafood Paella 96
State Fair Lamb Stew 79
Chicken Stock 24
chipotle chilies 76
chocolate
   Chocolate Bread Pudding with Coffee
      Liqueur 154
   Chocolate Meringue with Fresh
      Raspberries and Whipped Cream
      168, 169
   Chocolate Silk Pie 169
   Nighty-Night Cookies 157
chowder
   Midwestern Corn Chowder 73
   Schuler's Seafood Chowder 74
clams
   Schuler's Seafood Chowder 74
   Seafood Paella 96
Classic Coquille St. Jacques *88*, 89
cobbler, blueberry 171
cocktails 141-52
cocoa 154
Coconut Snowball *156*, 157
Coffee Cheesecake 160
Cognac Cherry Sauce 108
Cognac Peppercorn Sauce 109
cole slaw 37
condiments 24–30
cookies
   Lemon Dream Bars 158
   Nighty-Night Cookies 157
Coquille St. Jacques *88*, 89
corn
   Jalapeño Corn Bread 58

Midwestern Corn Chowder 73
Schuler's Seafood Chowder 74
Sweet Corn Tomato Sauce 127
corned beef brisket 62
cornmeal 57
Cosmopolitan 151
cottage cheese 130
crab
   Artichoke and Crab Stuffed
      Mushroom Caps 45
   Perfect Crab Cake 84
   Schuler's Seafood Chowder 74
crackers, whole wheat 52
cream cheese 48, 155, 160, 163
cream sauce
   Creole Mustard 29
   Dijon 100
   Horseradish 27
   Tomato Basil Cream Sauce 125
Creamy Sautéed Morel Mushrooms 57
crème de cocoa 161
crème de menthe 161
crème fraiche 155
Creole Mustard Sauce 29
Creole Seasoning 26
crostinis, 52
croutons, 35
crust
   bar cookie 158
   cheesecake 160
   pie 155
Crustless Spinach and Cheese Pie 130
cucumber 77, 92
Cucumber Sauce, Asian 86
Curried Chicken Salad with Fresh Fruit
   and Walnuts 32

daiquiri 152
desserts 153–171
Dijon Cream Sauce 100
dough, pizza 128
drinks 141–152
Dry Barbecue Rub 25

duck
   Duck and Wild Rice Salad 34
   Pan Roasted Duck Breast with Winter
      Vegetables 118
dumplings, spaetzle 140

eggplant
   Fried Eggplant with Boursin Cheese
      and Sweet Corn Tomato Sauce *126*,
      127
   Roasted Vegetable Panini 61
   Schuler's Signature Lasagna 123
eggs, Mushroom Omelet 122

Festive Carrot Ring 135
Filet of Beef with a Cognac Peppercorn
   Sauce 109
fish and seafood 83–98
   Fish Stock 25
   Schuler's Seafood Chowder 74
   Seviche and Avocado Salad 42
   See also specific types
flank steak 115
focaccia 53, 68
French Bistro Chicken with Tarragon
   Tomato Sauce *110*, 111
French Dip with Gruyère Cheese 70
Fresh Basil, Tomato and Camembert on
   Grilled Sourdough 66
Fried Eggplant with Boursin Cheese and
   Sweet Corn Tomato Sauce *126*, 127
fudge, Peppermint Ribbon Pie 163

garbanzo beans 47
garlic
   Garlic Crostini Chips 52
   Garlic and Herb Aioli 30
   Schuler's Garlic House Dressing 38
Gazpacho 77
gin 145
Goat Cheese Gratin 48
gouda cheese 64
graham cracker crust 160, 163, 169

Grandma Schuler's Cornish Pasties 103
Grandma's Pie Crust 155
Grasshopper Pie *9*, 161
green split peas 82
Grilled Salmon with Balsamic Vinegar
    Roasted Beets 91
Grilled Salmon Nicoise *36*, *37*
Grilled Sourdough Toast Points 52
ground round 46
Gruyère cheese 70, 73, 133

Halibut en Papillote 92
ham
    Ham and Roast Pork Panini 62
    Tortellini a la Crème with Ham and
        Mushrooms 121
    See also prosciutto
Hazelnut Crusted Walleye 87
Herbed Butter 29
Herbed Focaccia 53
herbs
    Baked Artichoke Hearts with Bread
        Crumbs and Fresh Herbs 56
    Cassoulet of Sausages 104
    Cauliflower with Lemon and Herb
        Butter 138
    Creole Seasoning 26
    Dijon Cream Sauce 100
    Garlic and Herb Aioli 30
    Herbed Butter 29
    Herbed Focaccia 53
    herbes de Provence 122
    Herb-Stuffed Trout with Horseradish
        Cream Sauce 98
    Lemon Herb Vinaigrette 39
    Mediterranean Roast Chicken 105
    Oven-Roasted Marinated Leg of Lamb
        112
    Schuler's Seasoning Salt 30
    See also basil
Herb-Stuffed Trout with Horseradish
    Cream Sauce 98
hors d'oeuvres and appetizers 43–58

Horseradish Cream Sauce 27
Hot Beef Brisket Sandwich with Smoked
    Gouda on Grilled Sourdough 64, *65*
Hot Mustard Sauce 28
House-Made Whole Wheat Crackers 52
hummus 61

ice cream
    Coconut Snowball 157
    Malted 161
    Peppermint Ribbon Pie 163

Jalapeño Corn Bread 58
jalapeño pepper 124
Jonathan's Barbecued Baby Back Ribs
    114
Jonathan's Soon-to-be-World Famous
    Margaritas *142*, 143

Kahlúa 154
Key Lime Pie 155

lamb
    Oven-Roasted Marinated Leg of Lamb
        112
    State Fair Lamb Stew 79
lasagna, vegetable 123
leeks, Baked Potato Soup 77
lemon 39, 148, 158
Lemon Dream Bars with Raspberry
    Coulis 158, *159*
Lemon Herb Vinaigrette 39
lima beans 82, 104
lime, 143, 155
liver, for pâté 50
lobster
    Lobster Paprikas 93
    Lobster and Peas with Saffron Pasta 94
London Broil 115
Lovers' Salad 35

Malted Ice Cream 161
Manhattan 145
Maple Syrup Dressing 38

margarita 143
marinade
  beef 102
  chicken 101, 105
  lamb 112
  London Broil 115
  ribs 114
Marinated Breast of Chicken Dakota 101
martini 145
Maytag blue cheese 68
meat and poultry 99–118. *See also beef,*
  chicken, pork
Meatballs, Schuler's Famous 46
Medallions of Veal with Scallions and
  White Wine Sauce 116, *117*
Mediterranean Roast Chicken with Pan
  Braised Potatoes 105
Mediterranean-Style Grilled Tuna Steak
  Hero 67
meringue 163, 169
Michigan Apple Crisp 167
Michigan Bean and Vegetable Soup 82
Michigan Country Apple Salad with
  Cheddar Cheese and Croutons 35
Midwestern Corn Chowder 73
mint 41, 138, 143
Mojito 143
morel mushrooms 57
mozzarella cheese 41, 123, 129
mushrooms
  Artichoke and Crab Stuffed
    Mushroom Caps 45
  Creamy Sautéed Morel Mushrooms 57
  Lobster Paprikas 93
  London Broil 115
  Mushroom Bisque 80
  Mushroom Omelet with Herbes de
    Provence and Asiago Cheese 122
  Roasted Vegetable Panini 61
  Savory Pesto Cheesecake 55
  Schuler's Signature Lasagna 123
  Tortellini a la Crème with Ham and
    Mushrooms 121
  Wild Mushroom Risotto 120

mussels
  Mussels in a White Wine Broth over
    Spaghetti 95
  Seafood Paella 96
mustard sauce
  Creole 29
  Hot 28
My Favorite Manhattan 145

navy beans 82
New England Pot Roast 115
Nicoise olives 37
Nighty-Night Cookies 157

olives, black 37, 67, 105
omelet, mushroom 122
onions
  Beef Short Ribs Braised in Red Wine
    102
  Midwestern Corn Chowder 73
  Potato Pancakes 140
  Roasted Vegetable Panini 61
  Schuler's Swiss Onion Soup 73
  Venison Ragout 78
orange 41, 148
Oreo cookie crumb crust 161, 163
Oven-Roasted Marinated Leg of Lamb
  112, *113*
oysters 57

Pan Roasted Duck Breast with Winter
  Vegetables 118
Pan Roasted Winter Vegetables 139
pancakes, potato 140
Pan-Fried Oysters with Spicy Remoulade
  Sauce 57
Pan-Fried Tuna Steak with an Asian
  Cucumber Sauce 86
panini
  Ham and Roast Pork 62
  Roasted Vegetable 61
paprika 93, 102
Parmesan cheese 55, 77, 104, 120, 121,
  123, 128

Party Sangria 148, *149*
pasta dishes
  Lobster and Peas with Saffron Pasta 94
  Mussels in a White Wine Broth over
    Spaghetti 95
  Radiator Pasta with Italian Sausage
    and Tomato Basil Cream Sauce 125
  Rotini Noodles with Shrimp, Red
    Peppers, and Sugar Snap Peas 130
  Summertime Vegetable Diablo with
    Angel Hair Pasta 124
pasties, meat 103
Pâté du Maison with a Rhubarb Port
  Wine Reduction 50, *51*
Peach Daiquiri 152
Peanut Butter Pie 163
peas
  Lobster and Peas with Saffron Pasta 94
  Michigan Bean and Vegetable Soup 82
  Rotini Noodles with Shrimp, Red
    Peppers, and Sugar Snap Peas 130
  Seafood Paella 96
pecans 157, 166
peppercorns, green 109
Peppermint Ribbon Pie 163
peppers, red 73, 74, 130
perch, Blackened Perch with Spicy
  Remoulade Sauce 84
Perfect Crab Cake with Creole Mustard
  Sauce 84, *85*
pesto
  Basil Pesto 27
  Prosciutto Pizza with Pesto and Sun-
    Dried Tomatoes 129
  Savory Pesto Cheesecake 55
pie
  Chocolate Silk 169
  Crustless Spinach and Cheese 130
  Grasshopper 161
  Key Lime 155
  Peanut Butter 163
  Peppermint Ribbon 163
  Strawberry Rhubarb 162

pie crust 155
pine nuts 27, 55, 137
pinto beans 82
pizza
    Prosciutto Pizza 129
    Quatro Formaggio Pizza 128
    Smoked Pork Pizza 129
Pizza Dough 128
Broiled Whitefish with Herbed Butter 90
pork
    Center Cut Pork Chops with a Dijon
        Cream Sauce 100
    Grandma Schuler's Cornish Pasties 103
    Ham and Roast Pork Panini 62
    Jonathan's Barbecued Baby Back Ribs
        114
    Schuler's Famous Meatballs 46
    See also ham, prosciutto
portabella mushroom 61
pot roast 115
Potato Pancakes 140
potatoes
    Baked Potato Soup 77
    Cheddar Mashed Potatoes 136
    Grandma Schuler's Cornish Pasties
        103
    Mediterranean Roast Chicken with
        Pan Braised Potatoes 105
    pancakes 140
    smashed 133
    Yukon Gold 91, 112, 133, 136
Potted Shrimp 49
poultry and meat 99–118. *See also beef,*
    chicken, pork
prime rib 68, 107
Prime Rib Sandwich with Sweet Onion
    Relish and Maytag Blue Cheese 68
prosciutto
    Cantaloupe and Prosciutto with Mixed
        Greens, Mint, and Mozzarella 41
    Prosciutto Cheese Straws 48
    Prosciutto Pizza with Pesto and Sun-
        Dried Tomatoes 129

provolone cheese 128
puff pastry 89
Pumpkin Bisque 80, *81*

Quatro Formaggio Pizza 128
Quiche Lorraine 120

Radiator Pasta with Italian Sausage and
    Tomato Basil Cream Sauce 125
ragout, Venison 78
raspberries 158, 169
Raspberry Coulis 158
red cabbage 132
red kidney beans 82
red peppers 73, 74, 130
red potatoes 105
red wine 148
remoulade sauce 30, 57, 84
reuben sandwich 62
rhubarb
    Pâté du Maison with a Rhubarb Port
        Wine Reduction 50
    Strawberry Rhubarb Pie 162
rib roast, 107
rice
    Duck and Wild Rice Salad 34
    Seafood Paella 96
    Wild Mushroom Risotto 120
ricotta cheese 128
risotto, Wild Mushroom Risotto 120
Roasted Asparagus with Pine Nuts 137
Roasted Garden Tomatoes *134*, 135
Roasted Vegetable Panini with
    Handmade Hummus and Feta Cheese
        60, 61
Rotini Noodles with Shrimp, Red
    Peppers, and Sugar Snap Peas 130
roux 73, 74, 80, 123
rubs 25
rum 143, 152
rutabaga 103
sake 152
Saketini 152
salad dressing 38–39

salads 31–42
    Bitter Green Salad with Sweet
        Potatoes, Bacon, and Oranges 41
    Brigadoon Salad 32
    Cole Slaw 37
    Curried Chicken Salad with Fresh
        Fruit and Walnuts 32
    Duck and Wild Rice Salad 34
    Lovers' Salad 35
    Michigan Country Apple Salad with
        Cheddar Cheese and Croutons 35
    Nicoise 37
    Schuler's Salad 32
    Seviche and Avocado Salad 42
salmon
    Grilled Salmon with Balsamic Vinegar
        Roasted Beets 91
    Grilled Salmon Nicoise 37
    Seviche and Avocado Salad 42
sandwiches 59-70
sausage
    Cassoulet of Sausages 104
    Radiator Pasta with Italian Sausage
        and Tomato Basil Cream Sauce 125
sauces
    Asian Cucumber 86
    Cognac Peppercorn 109
    Creole Mustard 29
    Dijon Cream 100
    Homemade Caramel Sauce 166
    Horseradish Cream, 27
    Hot Mustard 28
    Spicy Remoulade 30
    Sweet Corn Tomato 127
    Tomato Basil Cream Sauce 125
    White Wine 116
sauerkraut 62
Sautéed Summer Squash with Fresh
    Mint 138
Savory Pesto Cheesecake *54*, 55
scallops
    Classic Coquille St. Jacques 89
    Schuler's Seafood Chowder 74

Schuler's BBQ Sauce 26
Schuler's Classic Reuben Sandwich 62
Schuler's Famous Cole Slaw 37
Schuler's Famous Meatballs 46
Schuler's Famous Prime Rib *106*, 107
Schuler's Garlic House Dressing 38
Schuler's Heritage Cheese Spread 47
Schuler's Salad 32
Schuler's Seafood Chowder 74, *75*
Schuler's Seasoning Salt 30
Schuler's Signature Lasagna 123
Schuler's Swiss Onion Soup *72*, 73
seafood and fish 83–98
    Fish Stock 25
    Schuler's Seafood Chowder 74
    Seviche and Avocado Salad 42
    See also specific types
seasoning
    Creole 26
    salt 30
Seviche and Avocado Salad 42
shortcake, strawberry 170
shrimp
    Brigadoon Salad 32
    Potted Shrimp 49
    Rotini Noodles with Shrimp, Red
        Peppers, and Sugar Snap Peas 130
    Schuler's Seafood Chowder 74
    Seafood Paella 96
side dishes 131–140
Simple Syrup 143
Smoked Pork Pizza with Barbecue Sauce,
    Cheddar Cheese, and Scallions 129
soups
    Baked Potato Soup 77
    Beef Stock 24
    Chicken Stock 24
    Michigan Bean and Vegetable Soup 82
    Schuler's Swiss Onion Soup 73
    See also chowder
sourdough bread 52, 64, 66
South Haven Blueberry Cobbler 171
Spaetzle 140
Spicy Remoulade Sauce 30

spinach
    Crustless Spinach and Cheese Pie 130
    Schuler's Signature Lasagna 123
spreads
    cheddar cheese 47
    shrimp 49
squash
    Schuler's Signature Lasagna 123
    Summertime Vegetable Diablo with
        Angel Hair Pasta 124
    Sautéed Summer Squash with Fresh
        Mint 138
squid 96
State Fair Lamb Stew 79
stew, State Fair Lamb Stew 79
stocks
    Beef 24
    Chicken 24
stocks, rubs, and condiments 23–30
strawberries
    Strawberry Rhubarb Pie 162
    Strawberry Shortcake and Balsamic
        Vinegar Reduction 170
succotash, Summer Succotash 136
sugar snap peas 130
Simple Syrup 144
summer squash 123, 138
Summer Succotash 136
Summertime Vegetable Diablo with
    Angel Hair Pasta 124
Sweet Corn Tomato Sauce 127
Sweet and Sour House Dressing 39
sweet potatoes
    Avocado Sweet Potato Vichyssoise 76
    Bitter Green Salad with Sweet
        Potatoes, Bacon, and Oranges 41
Swiss cheese, 62, 120
syrup, simple 143

tahini 61
Tapenade Stuffed Cherry Tomatoes 56
tequila 143
toast points 52

Tomato Basil Cream Sauce 125
tomatoes
    Cassoulet of Sausages 104
    Fresh Basil, Tomato and Camembert
        on Grilled Sourdough 66
    Gazpacho 77
    juice 144
    Prosciutto Pizza with Pesto and Sun-
        Dried tomatoes 129
    Roasted Garden Tomatoes 135
    Rotini Noodles with Shrimp, Red
        Peppers, and Sugar Snap Peas 130
    State Fair Lamb Stew 79
    Sweet Corn Tomato Sauce 127
    Tapenade Stuffed Cherry Tomatoes 56
    Tarragon Tomato Sauce 111
Tortellini a la Crème with Ham and
    Mushrooms 121
trout, Herb-Stuffed Trout with
    Horseradish Cream Sauce 98
tuna
    Mediterranean-Style Grilled Tuna
        Steak Hero 67
    Pan-Fried Tuna Steak 86

veal, Medallions of Veal with Scallions
    and White Wine Sauce 116, 117
vegetable lasagna 123
vegetables
    Michigan Bean and Vegetable Soup 82
    Pan Roasted Duck Breast with Winter
        Vegetables 118
    Pan Roasted Winter Vegetables 139
    Schuler's Signature Lasagna 123
    Summer Succotash 136
    Summertime Vegetable Diablo 124
    See also specific vegetables
venison
    Pâté du Maison 50
    Venison Loin with a Cognac Berry
        Sauce 108
    Venison Ragout 78
vermouth 145

Vichyssoise, Avocado Sweet Potato 76
vinaigrette
    Balsamic Vinaigrette 39
    Lemon Herb Vinaigrette 39
vodka 125, 144, 151, 152

Walleye, Hazelnut Crusted 87
whiskey 145
white sauce 123
White Wine Sauce 116
whitefish
    Broiled Whitefish with Herbed Butter
        90
    Seviche and Avocado Salad 42
Whole Wheat Crackers 52
Wild Mushroom Risotto 120
wine, sangria 148

Yorkshire Pudding 133
Yukon Gold potatoes 91, 112, 133, 136
Yukon Gold Smashed Potatoes with
    Garlic and Chives 133

zucchini
    Fried Eggplant 127
    Roasted Vegetable Panini 61
    Schuler's Signature Lasagna 123
    Summertime Vegetable Diablo 124